First published by Carlton Books 2009

Copyright © Carlton Books Limited 2009

All rights reserved. No part of this publication may be reproduced, stored in a retrieval system, or transmitted in any form or by any means, electronic, mechanical, photocopying, recording or otherwise, without the prior permission of the copyright owner and the publishers.

The publisher has taken reasonable steps to check the accuracy of the facts contained herein at the time of going to press, but can take no responsibility for any errors.

Carlton Books Limited
20 Mortimer Street
London W1T 3JW

A CIP catalogue record for this book is available from the British Library

U.K Trade ISBN: 978-1-84732-271-5
U.K. Export ISBN: 978-1-84732-338-5

Commissioning Editor: Martin Corteel
Project Art Editor: Paul Chattaway
Editorial Assistant: David Ballheimer
Designer: Jake Davis
Picture Research: Paul Langan
Production: Kate Pimm

Printed in Dubai

Publisher's Notes
All statistics correct to the end of the 2008 Stanford Twenty20 challenge match, 1 November 2008.

About the author
CHRIS HAWKES, a former youth international and first-class cricketer with Leicestershire CCC (1990–92), is an experienced writer and editor, specializing in sport, who has worked on numerous titles for an array of publishers on an assortment of subjects. He lives in London.

Cricket Guide 2009

Chris Hawkes

CARLTON
BOOKS

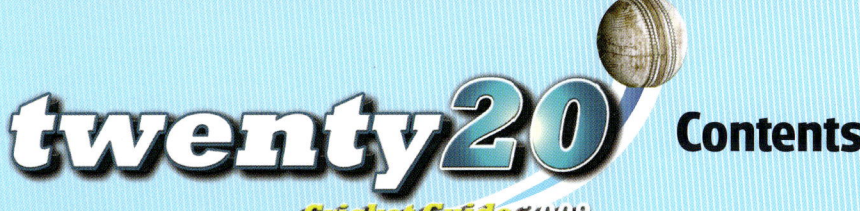

Contents

Introduction **8**

The Origins of Twenty20 **10**

The Top-20 Twenty20 Moments **14**

REVIEW OF THE SEASON 2007/08 **18**

ICC Twenty20 World Cup 2007 **20**

ICC World Twenty20 2009 Qualifiers **32**

The Rise of the Indian Premier League **34**

Indian Premier League 2008 **38**

Sir Allen Stanford – The US$20 Million-Dollar Game **48**

The Twenty20 Cup 2008 **52**

Women's Twenty20 **64**

Global Round-Up of Domestic Twenty20 Cricket **66**

PREVIEW OF THE SEASON 2009 **68**

ICC World Twenty20 2009 **70**

The Venues **72**

Group A: India **74**

Group A: Bangladesh **76**

Group B: Pakistan **78**

Group B: England **80**

Group C: Australia **82**

Group C: Sri Lanka **84**

Group C: West Indies **86**

Group D: New Zealand **88**

Group D: South Africa **90**

The Qualifiers **92**

Twenty20 World Cup 2009 Fill-in Chart **94**

Women's Twenty20 World Cup 2009 **96**

Twenty20 Cup 2009 **98**

Derbyshire · Durham · Essex · Glamorgan **100**

Gloucestershire · Hampshire · Kent · Lancashire **102**

Leicestershire · Middlesex · Northants · Nottinghamshire **104**

Somerset · Surrey · Sussex · Warwickshire **106**

Worcestershire · Yorkshire **108**

Indian Premier League 2009 **110**

Bangalore · Chennai · Deccan **112**

Delhi · Punjab · Kolkata **114**

Mumbai · Rajasthan **116**

Twenty20 Champions League 2008 **118**

Glossary / Rules and Regulations **120**

Statistics **122**

Picture Credits **128**

Introduction

Twenty20 cricket has a justifiable claim to being the fastest-growing spectator sport on the planet ... and a visit to a match is enough to explain why. This is the high-octane version of a much-loved game: spectacular strokeplay, athletic fielding, canny bowling and a result in three hours. In other words, every one of cricket's endearing qualities in a single evening out and a format, finally, that appeals to today's instant-gratification generation.

The real surprise is that Twenty20's spectacular rise took so long. Introduced in England in 2003 to provide a much-needed shot in the arm for a domestic cricket scene floundering on its knees, the new 20-over format was an instant hit attracting sell-out crowds. Other countries followed suit, with similar success stories, with the exception of a notable few, particularly India, in audience terms the global powerhouse of the game.

India's success in the 2007 World Twenty20 in South Africa – and the way Twenty20 stood up to prolonged exposure to a global audience for the first time – changed everything. India's cricket authorities, the BCCI (the most powerful board in world cricket), now had the hottest product in the sport, and, significantly, one that television companies were scrambling over themselves to get hold of. As a result, the Indian Premier League (IPL) was born.

The game had never seen anything like it. Multi-million-pound player auctions and previously unheard-of razzmatazz; it was the moment cricket met Bollywood; and it was an instant love affair. Over 3.4 million paying spectators flooded through the turnstiles for the IPL's 59 matches (an astonishing average of 58,000 per match), the action on the field of play was spectacular and, once again, cricket became the talk of the sporting world. Those watching with a more attentive eye knew the game could never be the same again.

Player auctions will become a season's highlight; 20-over tournaments will become a major part of the game's gossip; and big-money matches will become the norm. Twenty20 cricket is here to stay and the game will be the better for it. Existing television contracts may briefly halt its unstoppable march on the international game in the immediate future but, along with Test cricket, Twenty20 will become a staple of the international summer. The only remaining question is just how large a part of our cricketing diet it claims.

The challenge for cricket authorities around the world is to ensure that Test cricket remains the highest form of the game, the one in which young, aspiring cricketers dream of testing their skills. Test cricket has to remain the standard by which greatness should be measured. Twenty20 cricket is for the fans, the game's necessary moneymen and the players, who to a man will relish playing in it.

This book tells the story of what has been one of the most astonishing 18 months in cricket's long and distinguished history. Its intention is to hand every cricket fan the chance to get up to speed with this new and vibrant form of the game.

Chris Hawkes
December 2008

All-action entertainment: Twenty20 has seen the introduction of cheerleaders to many of the grounds.

A Marketing Man's Dream

Back in 2000, the England and Wales Cricket Board's head of marketing, Stuart Robertson, was handed the unenviable task of finding a solution to the ever-diminishing number of spectators passing through the turnstiles to watch English domestic cricket. Test and one-day international matches had been a sell-out success for years; in contrast, finding a seat at a county match had never been a problem.

His mission was not one born out of idle curiosity. The English counties had been surviving on ECB handouts for years and getting bums on seats was the only way to arrest the worrying, and financially draining, decline. The problem was, even the already small number of spectators was rapidly dwindling.

"The data we had was fairly black and white," said Robertson. "Attendances were down 20 per cent over five years." He and his team started to look for the reasons why and mobilized more than 30 focus groups, followed by 4,000 15-minute, one-on-one interviews, to gauge where the problem lay. Accessibility was the answer. "There was a physical reason – the timings of matches; people at work couldn't get to the game. But there was a cultural, social aspect, as well," Robertson continued. "A lot of people said: 'I thought you had to be a member to go to a game.'"

The solution to the malaise, a simple one, was 20-over cricket: a format that would see a result within three hours, so could be staged in the evenings – and which should appeal to the crucial 16–35 age group, the fanbase that had lifted football's financial fortunes in the late 1990s. The next problem was getting the idea past the county chairmen – traditionally a group not wholeheartedly committed to radical change. It may have been a sign of the times but, in 2001, recognizing the drastic need for a new direction, the suits representing the best interests of county cricket voted in favour of the concept – 11 votes to 7.

Top of the Pops: Atomic Kitten entertain the crowd at Trent Bridge on finals day in 2003.

A Marketing Man's Dream: The Origins of Twenty20

The Origins of Twenty20

Not everyone was convinced this was the direction cricket should be taking. The diehards said it would detract from the fundamental purity of the game, that cricket would be reduced to nothing more than an ugly slog. But similar arguments were thrown into the air when the game's ultimate cash cow, the one-day international, started to clog up the fixture list back in the late 1970s and early '80s. To the nay-sayers, this is what the greatest cricketer of all time, Sir Donald Bradman, had to say about one-day cricket and its detractors back in 1986: "It rids the game of the unutterable bore who thinks occupancy of the crease and personal aggrandisement are all that matter." It seems likely that cricket's greatest player would have been all in favour of Twenty20. The players, however, were less convinced.

"Like many, we took it as a bit of a joke to start with," said former Surrey captain Adam Hollioake. He was not alone. Leicestershire, like most of the county sides, held a practice match: the first side were bowled out inside 12 overs, a scene that would, no doubt, have been replicated across the country. Some players saw the Twenty20 Cup as a bit of fun; others saw it as a midsummer chance to recharge the batteries and opted out of proceedings altogether.

The first season was a huge hit. On the opening day of the inaugural Twenty20 Cup, auspiciously held on Friday, 13 July 2003, the authorities hoped to attract an average crowd of 2,400 spectators per ground – twice the gate for the domestic B&H Cup. The figures proved conservative: blessed by scorching weather, the crowds averaged a shade under 5,000 – and they were met by bouncy castles, face-painters, speed-daters, Jacuzzis, barbecue areas, rodeos ... and some pretty spectacular cricket, too.

Twenty20 cricket did not turn out to be the crash-bang-wallop affair many had feared. Well-crafted, cultured strokeplay, punctuated by the odd boundary, was more than enough to keep the scorecard ticking over. Even slow bowlers – tagged in most quarters before the competition as lambs to the slaughter in this form of the game – had a major, and decisive, role to play in the outcome of games. There were plenty of fireworks on display on the field of play, just not as many as people expected; but far from detracting from Twenty20's appeal, to the surprise of many, this merely added to it. Forget the gimmicks (and they would reduce over the years): Twenty20 cricket was more than big enough to stand up on its own two feet. South Africa's cricket authorities, who had been following events in England with eagle-eyed scrutiny, had seen enough and, in the winter of 2003–04, introduced their own domestic Twenty20 tournament: the Standard Bank Pro20 Series. It too was a runaway success. The challenge, however, lay in replicating that success year on year.

The English public's tremendous appetite for the 20-over game was confirmed when an average of 6,000 spectators per match turned out for

Loving it: The players loved it, and the crowds loved it, too. Twenty20 cricket was an instant hit in England in 2003.

A Marketing Man's Dream

the opening round of games at the 2004 Twenty20 Cup (1,000 up on the unexpectedly high figures of the previous year). On 15 July 2004 at Lord's – a ground which stands for all things traditional in the game – 27,500 people basked under the summer sunshine at cricket's venerable home to watch Middlesex's Twenty20 clash with Surrey. It was the largest turnout at a county match in England, barring domestic finals, since 1953.

Not surprisingly, the players too were starting to take the 20-over game more seriously. The competition provided them with an opportunity to parade their skills in packed stadiums and in a charged atmosphere usually reserved for one-day internationals and Test matches – an unheard-of prospect for the average county player even five years earlier. It was all a far cry from the three-jumper days at a windswept Scarborough in front of one man and his dog.

The 2005 Twenty20 Cup was proof, if further proof were needed, that domestic cricket had found a formula that provided a serious competition for the players and action-packed fun for the paying public. It had proved it could generate full stadiums week in, week out, and, most importantly of all, that it was a model that could be replicated around the world. But far beyond answering the need to provide much-needed funds for domestic cricket globally, the implications of just how far Twenty20 cricket could reach started to become abundantly clear to everyone involved with the game.

It was always going to be a slow process. Global cricket's fixture list – one that has been governed by pre-sold television rights for years – was already too congested to find anything other than the odd one-off game for cricket's little brother. New Zealand and Australia had played out the first 20-over international in Auckland on 17 February 2005. It was a poor-quality match and little more than a novelty affair. England's match against Australia at Southampton four months later, however, changed everything.

England, in front of a pumped-up partisan crowd, ran riot and won by 100 runs. The margin of victory almost certainly played a pivotal role in setting the tone for their Ashes heroics during the course of that memorable summer, but the game also had profound implications for Twenty20 cricket, most strikingly in the red-top newspapers' response to the game – the ultimate barometer of public opinion in the country.

"Thrashes!" screamed the back page of the punning *Sun*, at a time

Packing them in: All of a sudden the county pro was handed the chance to play in packed stadiums week in, week out.

A Marketing Man's Dream: The Origins of Twenty20

The Origins of Twenty20

when the football transfer rumour-mill usually occupies the majority of column inches. "Are they Bangladesh in disguise?" was the next question. Cricket had not been talked about in such terms for a long time – it was almost like following the national football team. Twenty20 cricket had captured the public's imagination. It had flexed its muscles on the international stage … and now it was not going to wait in the wings for long.

When the ICC first mooted the idea of staging a Twenty20 World Cup, 13 countries – including six of the big eight Test-playing nations – put their names forward as potential hosts. In the end the ICC decided that South Africa and England – the two countries that had first embraced Twenty20 cricket – would host the first two World Cups, with South Africa staging the first edition of the ICC World Twenty20 in September 2007.

The rush for tickets was intense, with many games – notably those involving South Africa, the semi-finals and the final – sold out in hours. The world's press listened intently, offering plenty of opinion, as competing teams announced their squads. ICC boss Ray Mali claimed Twenty20 cricket could well front the revolution to lead the game into China and the United States. Malcolm Speed, the ICC's chief executive, suggested that the tournament could provide the first step towards achieving his ultimate dream, to see India play a Test match against China.

The hype was intense. Cricket's little brother had won its chance to shine on the global stage and the pressure was on Twenty20 cricket to deliver.

Sold out: Middlesex's midweek Twenty20 showdown against Surrey on 15 July 2004 attracted a 27,500 full house, the largest crowd at a county match for more than 50 years.

The Making of a Giant: The Top-20 Twenty20 Moments

When the idea of a 20-over domestic cricket league was first mooted by the England and Wales Cricket Board back in 2000 it was greeted with equal measures of excitement and derision. But within eight years 20-over cricket had become one of the hottest sporting formulas on the planet. Here are 20 defining moments that have aided T20's metamorphosis from cricket's fledgling little brother into a giant of world sport.

1. ECB announce plans to launch a 20-over domestic tournament (2000)
The England and Wales Cricket Board discuss proposals to launch a domestic 20-over league in a desperate attempt to increase crowd levels. The talks, however, are abandoned. The idea resurfaces in 2001, and the domestic Twenty20 Cup is played out in 2003 – to great success and to packed stadiums.

2. Ian Harvey hits the first T20 century (23 June 2003)
Tension had been building. Seven rounds of matches had passed in the inaugural Twenty20 Cup and still no batsman had managed to pass the three-figure mark. That all changed on 23 June 2003 when Gloucestershire's veteran Australian all-rounder Ian Harvey smashed a match-winning unbeaten 50-ball 100 against Warwickshire.

3. Surrey win the inaugural Twenty20 Cup (19 July 2003)
A devastating spell of bowling from Surrey's James Ormond (4 for 11) reduced the inaugural Twenty20 Cup final, between Surrey and Warwickshire at a packed Trent Bridge, to a rather one-sided affair. Warwickshire slipped to 115 all out; Surrey cruised past the total in 10.5 overs to become the competition's first champions.

4. Andrew Symonds hits the fastest century in T20 history (2 July 2004)
On 2 July 2004, in the first round of matches of the second Twenty20 Cup, Australian all-rounder Andrew Symonds, playing for Kent, showed why he was destined to become one of 20-over cricket's most feared exponents. He dismantled the Middlesex bowling attack to reach three figures off 34 balls, hitting 16 fours and three sixes.

5. Dimitri Mascarenhas takes the first hat-trick in T20 history (9 July 2004)
On 9 July 2004, Sussex found themselves on the wrong end of some magnificent bowling by Hampshire's Dimitri Mascarenhas. The England all-rounder had already taken the wicket of Robin Martin-Jenkins, before returning to dismiss Brad Davis, Mushtaq Ahmed and Jason Lewry in successive deliveries to claim a T20 first.

6. First women's international match takes place at Hove (5 August 2004)
The 500 spectators who turned out at the county ground were in for a slice of history: the first-ever international T20 match, between England Women and New Zealand Women. And the result of the game hung in the balance until the final over, before New Zealand eventually ran out winners by nine runs.

7. First men's international takes place in Auckland (17 February 2005)
Within six months the men's game had followed suit, with New Zealand and Australia contesting the first men's T20 international in Auckland. A majestic unbeaten 55-ball 98 from Ricky Ponting hauled Australia to an impressive 214 for 5, before Michael Kasprowicz bagged 4 for 29 as New Zealand fell 44 runs short.

8. England beat Australia by 100 runs in first T20 international played on English soil (13 June 2005)
Billed as part of the countdown to the much-anticipated 2005 Ashes series, this match was the moment T20 cricket finally captivated the wider English public. A pumped-up England, defending a target of 179 and cheered on by a boisterous crowd, decimated the Australian line-up, bowling them out for 79 to win by a massive 100 runs.

9. Chris Gayle hits the first century in international T20 history
(11 September 2007) West Indies opener Chris Gayle got the 2007 ICC World Twenty20 off to a spectacular start, pummelling a bewildered South African attack to all parts of the Bullring in Johannesburg en route to a mesmerizing 117. He reached three figures – the first to do so in T20 international cricket – off just 50 balls.

10. Sri Lanka score a record 260 for 6 in their World Twenty20 match against Kenya (14 September 2007)
Sri Lanka stamped their authority over Kenya in record-breaking fashion in the opening match at the 2007 ICC World Twenty20. The islanders amassed a rollicking 260 for 6 in their 20 overs – a record in any form of T20 cricket. In reply, a bewildered Kenya slipped to 88 all out – the 172-run margin of victory is also a T20 record.

Blitzing the Boks: Chris Gayle blitzed the South African attack in the opening game of the World Twenty20 and became the first batsman to reach three figures in a T20 international.

The Making of a Giant: The Top-20 Twenty20 Moments

Treble trouble: Brett Lee takes the plaudits after becoming the first bowler in international T20 history to take a hat-trick, trapping Bangladesh's Alok Kapal LBW.

11. Brett Lee becomes the first bowler to take a hat-trick in an international T20 match (16 September 2007)
Brett Lee's express pace proved too much for the Bangladesh middle order. First Shakib al Hasan edged a catch behind; then Mashrafe Mortaza found his stumps flattened by a scorching yorker; and then Lee trapped Alok Kapal leg before. Bangladesh's innings lay in ruins. Lee had become the first man in T20 international history to claim a hat-trick.

12. Yuvraj Singh becomes first player to hit six sixes in an over in a T20 match (19 September 2007)
India's Yuvraj Singh had already despatched the first three balls of the 18th over for three massive sixes into the Durban stands. England's unfortunate Stuart Broad switched to bowling round the wicket. The same result: a six over backward point. Yuvraj crashed the fifth delivery over the mid-wicket boundary rope. And then came the coup de grace: roared on by the delirious crowd, he deposited the sixth ball over wide mid-on for the biggest maximum of them all. The Indian star had become the fourth player in history – and the first in T20 cricket – to hit six sixes in an over.

13. India become the first Twenty20 world champions (24 September 2007)
The dream final had come down to the last over. Pakistan needed 13 runs to win; India needed just a single wicket. Misbah-ul-Haq despatched Joginder Sharma's first ball for six, but then lost his nerve and holed out to short fine-leg. The Indian fairy-tale was complete: a billion people celebrated a victory that kick-started a chain of events that ensured cricket was never going to be the same again.

14. The Indian Cricket League is launched (30 November 2007)
The first edition of the Indian Cricket League – launched by Zee Telefilms – gets underway. Run parallel to an event endorsed by the Board of Control for Cricket in India, the league features six teams, with many paid overseas stars, with all matches played at Panchkula, Chandigarh. It is the first of three editions of the league to be played over the winter.

15. The start of the revolutionary player auction for the Indian Premier League (20 February 2008)
Bidding gets underway in the Hilton Towers hotel in Mumbai at the Indian Premier League's first player auction, and the pace is frenetic. A staggering US$7.175 million is paid out on ten players in the first two hours; by the end of the day the eight franchises had splashed out an eyebrow-raising US$34.955 million. Cricket had never seen anything like it.

16. Brendon McCullum gets the IPL off to a record-breaking start (18 April 2008)
It was a case of the action simply getting hotter after the Lord Mayor's Show. The Indian Premier League's opening ceremony may have been spectacular, but it could not compete with Brendon McCullum's innings for all-out action. The Kiwi, playing for Kolkata Knight Riders, smashed a magnificent unbeaten 158. The innings, which lasted 73 deliveries and contained 13 sixes and 10 fours, remains the highest individual score in T20 history.

17. Rajasthan's Sohail Tanvir records the best figures in T20 history (4 May 2008)
Called up by Pakistan as a late replacement for Shoaib Akhtar, Sohail Tanvir enjoyed a successful 2007 World Twenty20 with Pakistan. He went on to cement his reputation as one of the better exponents of the 20-over game by playing a starring role for the Rajasthan Royals, ending as the competition's leading wicket-taker with 22, including 6 for 14 against Chennai – the best bowling figures in T20 history.

18. Rajasthan Royals beat Chennai Super Kings to become inaugural Indian Premier League champions (1 June 2008)
Rajasthan Royals, the cheapest of the IPL's franchises at US$67 million and penalized for underbidding during the course of the auction, showed that money is not everything by becoming the Indian Premier League champions. The Royals, led by the irrepressible Shane Warne, and including some of the tournament's standout performers, such as Shane Watson and Sohail Tanvir, beat Chennai Super Kings by three wickets in the final in Mumbai.

19. Sir Allen Stanford announces US$1 million-a-man winner-takes-all showdown (12 June 2008)
Cricket had never seen anything like it. Texan billionaire Sir Allen Stanford landed his helicopter at Lord's and announced a series of five annual matches between the Stanford Superstars (players selected from domestic West Indies T20) and England. The prize-fund for the first match, on 1 November 2008, amounted to US$1 million to each player on the winning side – and nothing to the losers.

20. Essex's Graham Napier breaks the record for the most sixes in a T20 match (24 June 2008)
Graham Napier started the 2008 season as an undistinguished fringe member of the Essex squad and ended the year as one of the most talked-about players on the English domestic circuit. The reason: the former England A player smashed an unbeaten 152 against Sussex at Chelmsford. The innings – the second-highest score in T20 history – contained a world record 16 sixes.

Blast off: Brendon McCullum gets the IPL off to a blistering start with a world-record-breaking 158 not out for Kolkata Knight Riders against Bangalore Royal Challengers.

Review of the Season 2007/08

The months between September 2007 and September 2008 would provide at least three landmarks in Twenty20 cricket's history. First there was the inaugural ICC World Twenty20 in South Africa. Then there was the Indian Premier League with its Bollywood-style glamour, unprecedented player auctions, cheerleaders, a global television audience, and a unique type of inter-city cricket that captured the imagination of everyone involved in the game. Then the Twenty20 Cup continued to maintain its status as one of the sporting events of the English summer. It was quite a year for Twenty20 cricket: one that saw it evolve into a giant of world sporting events.

On top of the world: Jubilant Indian cricket team players raise the ICC World Twenty20 trophy after defeating Pakistan in the final at the Wanderers Cricket Stadium in Johannesburg, 24 September 2007.

ICC Twenty20 World Cup 2007

Unnecessarily drawn out, over-inflated ticket prices and half-empty stadiums: the 50-over-format World Cup held in the Caribbean between March and April 2007 had sapped the enthusiasm of even the most diehard cricket fan. Five months later, Twenty20 cricket had its chance to shine on the global stage. It passed with flying colours: cheap ticket prices saw packed stadiums, there were back-to-back matches, the cricket was spectacular and the tournament provided such a high level of entertainment that onlookers were left in no doubt that the 20-over format of the game will be around for a long time to come.

Cornucopia of colour: Images from the 2007 World Twenty20
Left: Fans waving flags from almost every team were on display at all the grounds;
Top: West Indies batsman Chris Gayle acknowledges the crowd on his way to a superb 117 against South Africa; Above: Fawad Alam (facing camera) is congratulated by Kamran Akmal as another New Zealand wicket falls in the semi-final.

ICC World Twenty20 2007

Twenty20 cricket, till September 2007 no more than a little brother brooding on the domestic fringes, had 14 days in the South African sun to flex its muscles in front of a global audience. The tournament was a massive hit and, although no one knew it at the time, it started a chain reaction that meant cricket would never be the same again.

Group A: (Bangladesh, South Africa, West Indies)

The tournament got off to a blistering start at the Wanderers. Chris Gayle, the West Indies captain, blasted a 57-ball 117 – the first century in international T20 history – to lead his side to an intimidating 205 for 6. But South Africa, roared on by a partisan crowd and aided by a woeful West Indian performance in the field, eased past the total with 14 balls to spare. Herschelle Gibbs, using a runner for most of his innings – and dropped twice – was the star of the show, hitting an unbeaten 90. The defeat highlighted the West Indies' inefficiencies with the ball, but it was their performance with the bat that let them down against Bangladesh. Gayle fell for a third-ball duck and a total of 164 for 8 always appeared vulnerable. Some inspired batting from Mohammad Ashraful (61) and Aftab Ahmed (62 not out) saw Bangladesh home with two overs to spare. The West Indies were out of the competition. It left a dead rubber between South Africa and Bangladesh, which the hosts – inspired by brothers Albie and Morne Morkel – won by seven wickets.

Qualified: South Africa (group winners) and Bangladesh

Group B: (Australia, England, Zimbabwe)

Australia had not played together since the World Cup final on 28 April 2007 and their rustiness showed against Zimbabwe. Aided by overcast conditions and a lively pitch, Zimbabwe – led by Elton Chigumbura (3 for 20) – restricted the much-vaunted Australian batsmen to 138 for 9. The hero of the Zimbabwe run-chase was Brendan Taylor, who hit an unbeaten 60 to guide his side to a memorable victory. Any celebrations were short-lived, however. The following day, Zimbabwe crashed to a Kevin Pietersen-inspired England by 50 runs and any chance of progress was out of their hands. An England win over Australia would send them through but, given their poor run-rate, an Australian win would send them crashing out of the tournament. Unfortunately for Zimbabwe, Australia bounced back from their humiliation in style, restricting England to 135 all out and, led by Matthew Hayden (67 not out) and Adam Gilchrist (45), galloping over the finishing line with more than five overs to spare. Australia were back in business. England, on the other hand, progressed to the second stage licking their wounds.

Qualified: Australia (group winners) and England

Group C: (Kenya, New Zealand, Sri Lanka)

New Zealand exploited the extra bounce on a well-grassed Durban pitch to send Kenya reeling. Mark Gillespie led the way with 4 for 7, Shane Bond chipped in with 2 for 12 (the best completed spell of bowling in T20 international history), and Kenya slumped to a record-low 73 all out. The Black Caps cantered to the target in just 7.3 overs. A switch to the more batsman-friendly Wanderers did little to change Kenyan fortunes. Sri Lanka, led by Sanath Jayasuriya at his ebullient best (44-ball 88), posted a record score of 260 for 6 to end the match as a contest. Kenya showed little taste for the fight and collapsed meekly to 88 all out. Kenya's early departure left a dead rubber between Sri Lanka and the Kiwis, but once more the Wanderers ground produced an entertaining encounter. New Zealand posted 164 for 7, before Jayasuriya blazed a trail once more (hitting a 44-ball 61) as Sri Lanka eased to the target with an over to spare. Jayasuriya and co. may have taken the honours on this occasion, but both sides had shown enough in the group stages to suggest they were serious contenders for the T20 World Cup crown.

Qualified: Sri Lanka (group winners) and New Zealand

Group D: (India, Pakistan, Scotland)

Pakistan needed a murderous performance from Shahid Afridi to see off a Scotland side that punched well above its weight. The one-day specialist butchered 22 from seven balls to take Pakistan to 171 for 9, and then proved equally destructive with the ball, taking 4 for 19, as the Scots slipped to 120 all out in reply. Persistent drizzle in Durban saw Scotland's next match, against a new-look India, abandoned without a ball being bowled. The no-result added further spice to the tournament's marquee match: India against Pakistan. A big win for Shoaib Malik's side could send India home early. Instead, the arch-rivals served up a classic. India struggled to 141 for 9 and needed to bowl and field well to have a chance. They did. Pakistan required a seemingly hopeless 39 from 15 deliveries when the dangerous Afridi fell in the 18th over

Host: South Africa (11–24 September 2007)

but, led by Misbah-ul-Haq (53), they reduced the target to 12 off the final over. Misbah-ul-Haq was run out trying to scramble a single off the final ball and the match ended in a tie. India won the bowl-out – surely an unnecessary gimmick – 3–0 to take the points.
Qualified: India (group winners) and Pakistan

SECOND PHASE

Group E: (England, India, New Zealand, South Africa)

New Zealand brushed aside the drubbing they had received against Sri Lanka in their final group game to beat India by five runs. Daniel Vettori was the star of the show, taking a match-winning 4 for 20 off his four overs as the Black Caps defended their total of 190. South Africa continued their unbeaten start to the tournament with a comfortable 19-run win over a misfiring England, who stuttered again two days later, against New Zealand in Cape Town. A magical four-wicket burst by Morne Morkel and some sensational power-hitting by Justin Kemp (56-ball 89) then handed South Africa a six-wicket win over New Zealand. It meant both South Africa and New Zealand would progress to the semi-finals if England could see off India in their final group game. They could not. Gautam Gambhir (58) and Virender Sehwag (68) got India off to a blistering start, but the real fireworks came towards the end of the innings. Yuvraj Singh became the first player in international T20 history – and the fourth in first-class cricket – to hit six sixes in an over (off the unfortunate Stuart Broad) en route to a 12-ball half-century as India posted a mighty 218 for 4. England made a good fist of the fight, but fell 18 runs short.

Group A

Team	P	W	L	T	NR	Pts	NetRR	For	Against
South Africa (Q)	2	2	0	0	0	4	+0.974	354/36.3	349/70.0
Bangladesh (Q)	2	1	1	0	0	2	+0.149	309/38.0	310/38.5
West Indies	2	0	2	0	0	0	–1.233	369/40.0	373/35.4

Group B

Team	P	W	L	T	NR	Pts	NetRR	For	Against
Australia (Q)	2	1	1	0	0	2	+0.987	274/34.5	274/39.5
England (Q)	2	1	1	0	0	2	+0.209	323/40.0	274/34.5
Zimbabwe	2	1	1	0	0	2	–1.196	277/39.5	326/40.0

Group C

Team	P	W	L	T	NR	Pts	NetRR	For	Against
Sri Lanka (Q)	2	2	0	0	0	4	+4.721	428/38.5	252/40.0
New Zealand (Q)	2	1	1	0	0	2	+2.396	238/27.4	241/38.5
Kenya	2	0	2	0	0	0	–8.047	161/40.0	334/27.4

Group D

Team	P	W	L	T	NR	Pts	NetRR	For	Against
India (Q)	2	0	0	1	1	3*	0.000	141/20.0	141/20.0
Pakistan (Q)	2	1	0	1	0	2	+1.275	312/40.0	261/40.0
Scotland	2	0	1	0	1	1	–2.550	120/20.0	171/20.0

* India won bowl-out against Pakistan 3–0

Group E

Team	P	W	L	T	NR	Pts	NetRR	For	Against
India (Q)	3	2	1	0	0	4	+0.750	551/60.0	506/60.0
New Zealand (Q)	3	2	1	0	0	4	+0.050	507/60.0	497/59.1
South Africa	3	2	1	0	0	4	–0.116	428/59.1	441/60.0
England	3	0	3	0	0	0	–0.700	494/60.0	536/60.0

Group F

Team	P	W	L	T	NR	Pts	NetRR	For	Against
Pakistan (Q)	3	3	0	0	0	6	+0.843	495/58.1	460/60.0
Australia (Q)	3	2	1	0	0	4	+2.256	390/44.1	389/59.1
Sri Lanka	3	1	2	0	0	2	–0.697	404/60.0	374/50.0
Bangladesh	3	0	3	0	0	0	–2.031	346/60.0	412/52.5

ICC World Twenty20 2007

India carried the momentum through to their must-win encounter against South Africa. Rohit Sharma (50 not out) and Mahendra Singh Dhoni (45) led them to 153 for 5, before some inspired bowling from RP Singh (4 for 13) saw South Africa crash to 116 for 9. India had romped through to the semi-finals, to be joined by New Zealand. South Africa, on the other hand, were left to lick their considerable wounds. Once again they had choked when it really mattered.
Qualified: India (group winners) and New Zealand

Group F: Australia, Bangladesh, Pakistan, Sri Lanka

Australia opened their second-phase campaign with a swift and brutal dismissal of Bangladesh. Bowling just short of a length to stifle the attacking instincts of the Bangladeshi batsmen, the Australian bowlers — led by Brett Lee, who recorded the first hat-trick in international T20 cricket — restricted Bangladesh to 123 for 8. Australia strolled to the target in the 14th over. Pakistan offered unbeaten Sri Lanka their toughest test of the tournament to date. Superb half-centuries from Shoaib Malik (57) and Younis Khan (51) took Pakistan to a formidable 189 for 6. It was all too much for Sri Lanka. Their much-vaunted top order failed to fire and then Shahid Afridi (3 for 18) choked the life out of any attempted comeback. Pakistan won by 33 runs and took the momentum into their clash with Australia the following day. Chasing 164 for 7, Misbah-ul-Haq (66 not out) and Shoaib Malik (52 not out) rescued Pakistan from a delicate 46 for 4 to guide them to a four-wicket win that effectively put them into the semi-finals. Sri Lanka kept their hopes of progress alive with a crushing 64-run win over hapless Bangladesh to set up a winner-takes-all clash with Australia. It was a dramatically one-sided affair. Sri Lanka opted for a gung-ho approach to batting and paid the price, slipping to 43 for 7 — with Stuart Clark taking 4 for 20 — before recovering to 101 all out. Matthew Hayden (58 not out) and Adam Gilchrist (31 not out) showed the Sri Lankans just how wrong their approach had been; calm, measured ball-striking took them to the target after a mere 10.2 overs. Pakistan earned their third successive victory with a hard-fought, if not entirely convincing, four-wicket win over Bangladesh. The tournament may only have been 11 days old, but we had already reached the sharp end of it.
Qualified: Pakistan (group winners) and Australia

SEMI-FINALS

Semi-Final One
22 September 2007 at Newlands, Cape Town
New Zealand 143 for 8 (20 overs) (Umar Gul 3 for 15)
Pakistan 147 for 4 (18.5 overs) (Imran Nazir 59)
Pakistan won by six wickets

Pakistan's bowling attack had been one of the revelations of the tournament. Sohail Tanvir had gone for less than seven runs an over; leg-spinner Shahid Afridi's bag of tricks had kept the batsmen under control; and Umar Gul, one of the lesser lights of the Pakistan squad, was turning out to be one of the bowlers of the tournament. Gul was at it again during the first semi-final in Cape Town. After 10 overs, New Zealand (on 70 for 1) had built a solid base from which to attack. Gul came on and took 3 for 15 to restrict New Zealand to 143 for 8 when a total of 160-plus seemed more likely. Pakistan, led by 59 from Imran Nazir, cantered to the target with seven balls to spare. Yet again New Zealand had fallen at the semi-final stage of a major international tournament. Pakistan, on the other hand, were through to their first final since their 1999 World Cup defeat to Australia. This time they would be looking to go one better.

Semi-Final Two
22 September 2007 at Kingsmead, Durban
India 188 for 5 (20 overs) (Yuvraj Singh 70)
Australia 173 for 7 (20 overs) (ML Hayden 62)
India won by 15 runs

India's fairy-tale progress through the tournament continued when they put in a mesmerizing all-round performance against Australia. Little-fancied at the start of the competition, India's progress had been based on team-work, and once again individuals performed at just the right moments. With only 48 runs on the board (for two wickets) after the first 10 overs, things could have been very different, but then Yuvraj Singh, supported ably by Mahendra Singh Dhoni, produced yet another memorable knock — 70 off 30 balls — and India hauled themselves to a formidable 188 for 5. Australia made a keen fight of the chase and by the 14th over — with Matthew Hayden and Andrew Symonds having added 66 in six overs — were favourites to win. Then Sreesanth, who had already accounted for Gilchrist in his first spell, returned to remove Hayden. The Australian juggernaut was halted. Sreesanth ended with the remarkable figures of 4-1-12-2, Australia fell 15 runs

Victory charge: India's young guns pour on to the pitch after clinching victory over Pakistan in the inaugural World Twenty20 final in Johannesburg.

short of the target and, magically, India were through to the final.

ICC WORLD TWENTY20 FINAL
India v Pakistan at New Wanderers Stadium, Johannesburg

Both sides had enjoyed a dream run to the final. India's assembled mix of players – without Sachin Tendulkar, Sourav Ganguly and Rahul Dravid – had defied their own low pre-tournament expectations; Pakistan had risen from the horrors of their World Cup campaign in the West Indies – one that had seen the sudden and mysterious death of their coach Bob Woolmer; and cricketing administrators were rubbing their hands together in glee at the prospect of a match that would capture the attention of a global cricket audience. Ten days earlier in Durban the two sides had played out a tie. This time round they served up a classic.

India were forced to work hard for their runs. Gautam Gambhir (75) and Umar Gul (3 for 28) shared the honours and it required a late 30-run cameo from Rohit Sharma to haul India up to a total of 157 for 5. It seemed a below-par performance. But then India's bowlers set to work. Irfan Pathan (3 for 16) was magnificent, RP Singh (3 for 26) provided commendable support and with Pakistan requiring 54 runs off the final 24 deliveries with three wickets in hand, India seemed to have the match in their grasp. Misbah-ul-Haq had other ideas, swiping Harbhajan for three sixes. With one over remaining, Pakistan required 13 runs with one wicket in hand and Misbah on strike. Mahendra Singh Dhoni threw the ball to the inexperienced Joginder Sharma. The first ball was a wide; the second was despatched over long-on for six; on the next ball Misbah made a curious shot selection and was caught at short fine-leg. India had held their nerve when it mattered most: they had become the newly crowned Twenty20 world champions.

FINAL
24 September 2007 at New Wanderers Stadium, Johannesburg
India beat Pakistan by five runs

India			R	B	4s	6s	SR
G Gambhir	c Asif	b Umar Gul	75	54	8	2	138.88
YK Pathan	c Shoaib Malik	b Asif	15	8	1	1	187.50
RV Uthappa	c Afridi	b Sohail Tanvir	8	11	1	0	72.72
Yuvraj Singh	c & b	Umar Gul	14	19	1	0	73.68
†*MS Dhoni		b Umar Gul	6	10	0	0	60.00
RG Sharma		not out	30	16	2	1	187.50
IK Pathan		not out	3	3	0	0	100.00
Extras	(lb 1, w 4, nb 1)		7				
Total	(5 wickets, 20 overs)		157				

Fall of wickets: 1-25, 2-40, 3-103, 4-111, 5-130
Did not bat: Harbhajan Singh, Joginder Sharma, RP Singh
Bowling: Mohammad Asif 3-0-25-1; Sohail Tanvir 4-0-29-1; Shahid Afridi 4-0-30-0; Mohammad Hafeez 3-0-25-0; Umar Gul 4-0-28-3; Yasir Arafat 2-0-19-0

Pakistan			R	B	4s	6s	SR
Moham'd Hafeez	c Uthappa	b Singh	1	3	0	0	33.33
Imran Nazir	run out	(Uthappa)	33	14	4	2	235.71
†Kamran Akmal		b Singh	0	3	0	0	0.00
Younis Khan	c YK Pathan	b J Sharma	24	24	4	0	100.00
*Shoaib Malik	c Sharma	b IK Pathan	8	17	0	0	47.05
Misbah-ul-Haq	c Sreesanth	b J Sharma	43	38	0	4	113.15
Shahid Afridi	c Sreesanth	b IK Pathan	0	1	0	0	0.00
Yasir Afafat		b IK Pathan	15	11	2	0	136.36
Sohail Tanvir		b Sreesanth	12	4	0	2	300.00
Umar Gul		b Singh	0	2	0	0	0.00
Mohammad Asif		not out	4	1	1	0	400.00
Extras	(b 1, lb 4, w 6, nb 1)		14				
Total	(all out, 19.3 overs)		152				

Fall of wickets: 1-2, 2-26, 3-53, 4-65, 5-76, 6-77, 7-104, 8-138, 9-141, 10-152
Bowling: RP Singh 4-0-26-3; S Sreesanth 4-1-44-1; Joginder Sharma 3.3-0-20-2; YK Pathan 1-0-5-0; IK Pathan 4-0-16-3; Harbhajan Singh 3-0-36-0

Umpires: MR Benson (England) and SJA Taufel (Australia)
Man of the Match: IK Pathan (India)
Player of the Series: Shahid Afridi (Pakistan)

ICC World Twenty20 2007

Mr Maximum: India's Yuvraj Singh becomes the first player in international Twenty20 cricket history to hit six sixes in an over, off Stuart Broad of England.

HONOURS BOARD

TEAM HONOURS

Highest Total

Total	Team	Overs	RR	Inns	Opposition	Venue	Date
260/6	Sri Lanka	20.0	13.00	1	Kenya	Johannesburg	14/09/2007

Biggest Margin of Victory – by runs

Margin	Winner	Target	Opposition	Venue	Date
172 runs	Sri Lanka	261	Kenya	Johannesburg	14/09/2007

By Wickets

Margin	Winner	Balls Rem	Target	Overs	Opposition	Venue	Date
10 wkts	Australia	58	102	10.2	Sri Lanka	Cape Town	20/09/2007

INDIVIDUAL HONOURS

Most Runs

Player	M	I	NO	Runs	HS	Ave	BF	SR	100	50
ML Hayden (Aus)	6	6	3	265	73*	88.33	183	144.80	0	4
G Gambhir (Ind)	7	6	0	227	75	37.83	175	129.71	0	3
Misbah-ul-Haq (Pak)	7	7	3	218	66*	54.50	156	139.74	0	2
Shoaib Malik (Pak)	7	7	2	195	57	39.00	154	126.62	0	2
KP Pietersen (Eng)	5	5	0	178	79	35.60	110	161.81	0	1
JM Kemp (SA)	5	5	3	173	89	86.50	124	139.51	0	1
AC Gilchrist (Aus)	6	6	1	169	45	33.80	112	150.89	0	0
CD McMillan (NZ)	6	5	1	163	57	40.75	80	181.11	0	1
Aftab Ahmed (Bang)	5	5	1	162	62*	40.50	125	129.50	0	1
DPMD Jayawardene (SL)	5	5	1	159	65	39.75	104	152.88	0	1

Highest Score

Player	Runs	Balls	4s	6s	SR	Team	Opposition	Venue	Date
CH Gayle	117	57	7	10	205.26	West Indies	South Africa	Johannesburg	11/09/2007
HH Gibbs	90*	55	14	2	163.63	South Africa	West Indies	Johannesburg	11/09/2007
JM Kemp	89*	56	6	6	158.92	South Africa	New Zealand	Durban	19/09/2007
ST Jayasuriya	88	44	11	4	200.00	Sri Lanka	Kenya	Johannesburg	14/09/2007
KP Pietersen	79	37	7	4	213.51	England	Zimbabwe	Cape Town	13/09/2007
G Gambhir	75	54	8	2	138.88	India	Pakistan	Johannesburg	24/09/2007
ML Hayden	73*	48	9	3	152.08	Australia	Bangladesh	Cape Town	16/09/2007
Junaid Siddique	71	49	6	3	144.89	Bangladesh	Pakistan	Cape Town	20/09/2007
Yuvraj Singh	70	30	5	5	233.33	India	Australia	Durban	22/09/2007
V Sehwag	68	52	4	3	130.76	India	England	Durban	19/09/2007

Most Sixes

Player	Innings	Sixes
CD McMillan (New Zealand)	5	13
Yuvraj Singh (India)	5	12
CH Gayle (West Indies)	2	10
JM Kemp (South Africa)	5	10
ML Hayden (Australia)	6	10
Imran Nazir (Pakistan)	7	10
Misbah-ul-Haq (Pakistan)	7	9
JA Morkel (South Africa)	3	7
ST Jayasuriya (Sri Lanka)	5	7
LRPL Taylor (New Zealand)	5	7
AC Gilchrist (Australia)	6	7

Great start: Chris Gayle smashes 117 against South Africa.

ICC World Twenty20 2007

Most Wickets

Player	Mat	O	M	Runs	Wkts	BBI	Ave	Econ	SR	4w	5w
Umar Gul (Pakistan)	7	27.4	0	155	13	4/25	11.92	5.60	12.7	1	0
SR Clark (Australia)	6	24.0	0	144	12	4/20	12.00	6.00	12.0	1	0
RP Singh (India)	7	24.0	0	152	12	4/13	12.66	6.33	12.0	1	0
Shahid Afridi (Pakistan)	7	28.0	1	188	12	4/19	15.66	6.71	14.0	1	0
DL Vettori (New Zealand)	6	24.0	0	128	11	4/20	11.63	5.33	13.0	1	0
IK Pathan (India)	7	22.0	1	149	10	3/16	14.90	6.77	13.2	0	0
Mohammad Asif (Pakistan)	7	26.5	0	212	10	4/18	21.20	7.90	16.1	1	0
M Morkel (South Africa)	5	20.0	0	120	9	4/17	13.33	6.00	13.3	1	0
NW Bracken (Australia)	6	22.2	0	142	8	3/16	17.75	6.35	16.7	0	0
MG Johnson (Australia)	6	24.0	0	153	8	3/22	19.12	6.37	18.0	0	0

Best Bowling in an Innings

Player	O	M	R	W	Econ	Team	Opposition	Venue	Date
MR Gillespie	2.5	0	7	4	2.47	New Zealand	Kenya	Durban	12/09/2007
RP Singh	4.0	0	13	4	3.25	India	South Africa	Durban	20/09/2007
M Morkel	4.0	0	17	4	4.25	South Africa	New Zealand	Durban	19/09/2007
Mohammad Asif	4.0	0	18	4	4.50	Pakistan	India	Durban	14/09/2007
Shahid Afridi	4.0	0	19	4	4.75	Pakistan	Scotland	Durban	12/09/2007
DL Vettori	4.0	0	20	4	5.00	New Zealand	India	Johannesburg	16/09/2007
SR Clark	4.0	0	20	4	5.00	Australia	Sri Lanka	Cape Town	20/09/2007
Umar Gul	4.0	0	25	4	6.25	Pakistan	Scotland	Durban	12/09/2007
E Chigumbura	4.0	0	31	4	7.75	Zimbabwe	England	Cape Town	13/09/2007
Shakib Al Hasan	4.0	0	34	4	8.50	Bang'desh	West Indies	Johannesburg	13/09/2007

Hot hand: Pakistan's Umar Gul had an impressive tournament with the ball.

Best Economy Rate (qualification 4 wickets)

Player	O	M	R	W	BBI	Ave.	Econ	4w	5w
DL Vettori (New Zealand)	24.0	0	128	11	4/20	11.63	5.33	1	0
WPUJC Vaas (Sri Lanka)	18.0	1	100	5	2/14	20.00	5.55	0	0
Umar Gul (Pakistan)	27.4	0	155	13	4/25	11.92	5.60	1	0
SR Clark (Australia)	24.0	0	144	14	4/20	12.00	6.00	1	0
M Morkel (South Africa)	20.0	0	120	9	4/17	13.33	6.00	1	0
A Flintoff (England)	18.0	0	110	5	2/23	22.00	6.11	0	0
CRD Fernando (Sri Lanka)	17.0	3	104	6	2/17	17.33	6.11	0	0
RP Singh (India)	24.0	0	152	12	4/13	12.66	6.33	1	0
NW Bracken (Australia)	22.2	0	142	8	3/16	17.75	6.35	0	0
Abdur Razzak (Bang'desh)	19.0	0	121	7	2/16	17.28	6.36	0	0

Quick strike: Bangladesh bowler Syed Rasel has just dismissed Chris Gayle with the third ball of the West Indies innings.

Twenty20 World Cup Team of the Tournament

1. Matthew Hayden (Australia)
265 runs (ave: 88.33; strike rate: 144.80)
A rock at the top of the Australian order in Test and 50-over cricket for the best part of a decade, the 36-year-old Queenslander unveiled all his skills in the 20-over format of the game and ended up the tournament's leading run-scorer (265 runs). He contributed four half-centuries to the Australian cause – three of them unbeaten match-winning efforts – and his 62 in the semi-final against India almost dragged his side through to the final.

2. Gautam Gambhir (India)
227 runs (ave: 37.83; strike rate: 129.71)
India's most consistent batsman during the course of their successful campaign, Gautam Gambhir used the ICC World Twenty20 as a personal springboard in his attempt to secure a permanent place in the Indian side. The left-handed opener did a magnificent job, scoring three half-centuries, and ended the tournament as the second-highest run-scorer. His brilliant 75 in the final against Pakistan did much to help his country to the World Twenty20 crown.

3. Chris Gayle (West Indies)
117 runs (ave: 58.50; strike rate: 195.00)
Chris Gayle's tournament may have been a brief affair – indeed, the second of his two innings lasted a mere three balls – but when he fired, the West Indies captain showed exactly why he has a reputation of being one of the most destructive power-hitters in the game. He set the tournament alight in the opening game when he smashed a 57-ball 117 – the first century in international T20 cricket history.

4. Yuvraj Singh (India)
148 runs (ave: 29.60; strike rate: 194.73)
His contributions may not have been as consistent as the Indian management team would have desired, but Yuvraj Singh produced two performances that captured the global headlines. The first came against England, when the mercurial left-hander smashed a 12-ball half-century, including six sixes off one Stuart Broad over; the second came in the semi-final when his inspired 30-ball 70 took the game out of Australia's reach.

5. Misbah-ul-Haq (Pakistan)
218 runs (ave: 54.50; strike rate: 139.74)
One momentary lapse in the final apart, Misbah-ul-Haq's performances in the ICC World Twenty20 did much to silence the critics who had questioned the 34-year-old's inclusion in the Pakistan squad at the expense of the prolific Mohammad Yousuf. The veteran one-day specialist was the tournament's third-highest run-scorer, hitting two

Matthew Hayden: Australia may have endured a disappointing tournament, but their prolific Queensland opener was in mesmeric form with the bat.

half-centuries including a match-winning 66 not out against Australia. His performances earned him a recall to the Pakistan Test side.

6. Mahendra Singh Dhoni (India, captain/wicketkeeper)
154 runs (ave: 30.80; strike rate: 128.33)
An inspirational choice as captain and the new golden boy of Indian cricket, Mahendra Singh Dhoni cajoled the very best out of an Indian squad lacking Sachin Tendulkar, Rahul Dravid and Sourav Ganguly. He also made some vital contributions with the bat, hitting 154 runs in the competition, including 45 in India's must-win encounter against South Africa and a crucial 36 (off 18 balls) in his side's 15-run semi-final win over Australia.

7. Shahid Afridi (Pakistan)
91 runs (ave: 15.16; strike rate: 197.82); 12 wickets (ave: 15.66; economy: 6.71)
The player of the tournament, Shahid Afridi was born to play Twenty20 cricket. A whirling dervish with the bat, he hit a seven-ball 22 against Scotland and a 15-ball 39 against Bangladesh. He also made some stifling contributions with the ball. Showing great variety – leg-spinners, top-spinners, googlies and fast balls – he took 12 wickets during the competition at an economy rate of 6.90, including a match-winning 4 for 19 in Pakistan's tournament-opening match against Scotland.

8. Daniel Vettori (New Zealand)
36 runs (ave: 9.00; strike rate: 180.00); 11 wickets (ave: 11.63; economy: 5.33)
Daniel Vettori adapted to the New Zealand captaincy following the retirement of Stephen Fleming with characteristic ease. The 29-year-old left-armer also showed why slow bowlers have such an important role to play in Twenty20 cricket. He took 11 wickets in seven matches, including an impressive and match-winning 4 for 20 against India in the second phase, and his economy rate of 5.33 was the best in the tournament.

9. Irfan Pathan (India)
34 runs (ave: 17.00; strike rate: 113.33); 10 wickets (ave: 14.90; economy: 6.77)
Irfan Pathan may only have taken 10 wickets during the tournament at an economy rate of 6.77, but the man many consider to be the best seam and swing bowler India has produced since Kapil Dev came to life when it really mattered. His spell of 3 for 16 in the final against Pakistan was a major factor behind India's ICC World Twenty20 success and a performance that earned him the Man of the Match award.

10. Stuart Clark (Australia)
12 wickets (ave: 12.00; economy: 6.00)
Such was the unerring, metronomic accuracy of Stuart Clark throughout the ICC World Twenty20 that Australia barely noticed the absence of the newly retired Glenn McGrath for the first time in a major tournament since 1996. The 32-year-old New South Wales paceman was in majestic form with the ball, bagging 12 wickets – including a match-winning 4 for 20 against Sri Lanka – with an impressive economy rate of 6.00 runs per over.

11. Umar Gul (Pakistan)
13 wickets (ave: 11.92; economy: 5.60)
Much of the pre-tournament brouhaha revolved around Shoaib Akhtar's expulsion from the Pakistan squad following a dressing-room scuffle with Mohammad Asif, but a string of stellar performances from Umar Gul ensured the Rawalpindi Express was not missed. Two three-wicket hauls (in the semi-final and final) and a match-winning 4 for 25 against Scotland saw him end as the tournament's leading wicket-taker (with 13), and all at an impressive economy rate of 5.60.

Mahendra Singh Dhoni: The Indian wicketkeeper proved to be an astute choice as captain. He made some telling contributions with the bat, was his usual self behind the stumps and skippered his team all the way to victory in the final against Pakistan.

ICC World Twenty20 2009 Qualifiers

The announcement in July 2008 that Zimbabwe had withdrawn from the 2009 ICC World Twenty20 event in England left a simple equation. The six top-rated Associate teams would fight it out for the now three remaining places in Belfast, Northern Ireland, from 2 to 5 August 2008.

The six teams were split into two groups – Group A (Ireland, Scotland, Bermuda) and Group B (Kenya, Netherlands, Canada) – with the top two teams from each group progressing to the semi-finals. The winners of the semis would secure two of three World Twenty20 spots with the losing teams left to battle it out for the one remaining berth. The smart money was on Kenya, the shock 2003 World Cup semi-finalists, and Ireland, who had surpassed expectations with a surprise win over Pakistan in the 2007 World Cup, with Scotland and the Netherlands left to fight over third place. Things, however, did not quite work out like that.

Scotland got off to the worst possible start, coming out on the wrong side of a low-scoring, last-ball thriller against Ireland in the opening Group A encounter, but they rescued their tournament in style with a comfortable eight-wicket win over Bermuda, leaving the islanders needing to beat Ireland in the final group match to keep their tournament hopes alive. Bermuda lost a frenzied, almost farcical, nine-over rain-affected slog by four runs.

The Netherlands, led by Essex all-rounder Ryan ten Doeschate (56 and 3 for 27), kicked off their Group B campaign in style, shocking Kenya with a 19-run win, but their joy turned into despair later in the day when they slipped to 97 all out against Canada and lost by four wickets. The next day it was Canada's turn to discover just how quickly fortunes can change in Twenty20 cricket: a four-wicket defeat to Kenya left them out of the chase for the tournament's major prize.

Kenya scraped through to the semi-finals on run-rate, behind group winners the Netherlands. But their struggles with the bat continued in their semi-final clash against Ireland. Dismissed for a paltry 67, the hosts passed the target with four wickets and five balls to spare. It may not have been one of Ireland's prettiest wins, but it was mission accomplished. They had become the first team to secure a berth at the 2009 ICC World Twenty20.

A few hours later they were joined by the Netherlands, who came out on top of their last-four encounter with Scotland. After ten overs it had all looked so good for the Scots. They were 50 for 0 and cruising, before slipping to an abject 107 for 8. The Netherlands eased to the target with a full two overs to spare.

All was not lost for Scotland, however. Later in the day they squared off against Kenya in a winner-takes-all encounter for the final World Twenty20 berth. The Scots won the spoils, restricting Kenya to 106 for 9, and, led by captain Ryan Watson (54 not out), reached the target with 11 balls to spare to secure a nine-wicket win.

Rain left the tournament ending on a damp note, with the final between Ireland and the Netherlands abandoned without a ball being bowled. The trophy was shared, but the tournament's major prizes had already been won.

All-round star: AC Botha starred with bat and ball in Ireland's semi-final win over Kenya.

32 ICC World Twenty20 2009 Qualifiers

Group A

Team	P	W	L	T	NR	Pts	NetRR	For	Against
Ireland	2	2	0	0	0	4	+0.205	163/28.5	158/29.0
Scotland	2	1	1	0	0	2	+0.313	217/37.4	217/39.5
Bermuda	2	0	2	0	0	0	-0.610	140/29.0	145/26.4

Group B

Team	P	W	L	T	NR	Pts	NetRR	For	Against
Netherlands	2	1	1	0	0	2	+0.351	250/40.0	233/39.3
Kenya	2	1	1	0	0	2	-0.126	226/37.5	244/40.0
Canada	2	1	1	0	0	2	-0.185	190/39.3	189/37.5

First semi-final
4 August 2008 at Stormont, Belfast
Kenya 67 (17.2 overs) (AC Botha 3 for 20)
Ireland 72 for 6 (19.1 overs) (AC Botha 22)
Ireland beat Kenya by four wickets
Ireland qualify for 2009 ICC World Twenty20
Group A (alongside India and Bangladesh)

Second semi-final
4 August 2008 at Stormont, Belfast
Scotland 107 for 8 (20 overs) (KJ Coetzer 40, RN ten Doeschate 3 for 23)
Netherlands 110 for 5 (18 overs)
(ES Szwarczynski 30)
Netherlands beat Scotland by five wickets
Netherlands qualify for 2009 ICC World Twenty20
Group B (alongside Pakistan and England)

Third-place playoff
4 August 2008 at Stormont, Belfast
Kenya 106 for 9 (20 overs) (JD Nel 3 for 10)
Scotland 107 for 1 (18.1 overs)
(RR Watson 54 not out, KJ Coetzer 48)
Scotland won by nine wickets
Scotland qualify for 2009 ICC World Twenty20
Group D (alongside New Zealand and South Africa)

Final
5 August 2008 at Stormont, Belfast
Ireland v Netherlands
Match abandoned without a ball being bowled – trophy shared

Elementary: Scotland captain Ryan Watson led from the front with the bat in the third-place play-off to secure for his team the final qualifying berth for the 2009 Twenty20 World Cup.

The Rise of the Indian Premier League

India's unexpected success in the World Twenty20 in South Africa led to scenes of unprecedented joy in a cricket-mad nation containing over one billion diehard fans. It also gave the Board of Control for Cricket in India (BCCI) – world cricket's most powerful administrative body – an opportunity to put an irritating upstart in its place.

It may have been the last country to accept Twenty20 cricket on a domestic level, but the shadow of the 20-over game had hung over Indian cricket for some time and the root of it lay in the BCCI's distribution of television rights. Back in 2003, Zee Telefilms (part of the Essel Group promoted by rice-trader-turned-media-baron Subash Chandra) bid for the television rights for that year's World Cup in South Africa. It was the highest offer, but the BCCI rejected it. Zee tried again in 2004 and, despite ending up in court, lost out once more. The same thing happened two years later. In April 2007, with television time at his disposal and with content needed to fill it, Chandra declared he was going to launch a Twenty20 competition called the Indian Cricket League (ICL).

Chandra wrote to the BCCI explaining his intentions to set up a league that would run parallel with, and not in opposition to, any 20-over tournament planned by the BCCI. The governing body's initial response was lukewarm, at best. The reaction in the Indian media, however, was mixed. India had just endured a humiliating early exit from the 50-over World Cup in the Caribbean – including embarrassing reverses to Bangladesh and Sri Lanka – and that after having suffered a frustrating 2–1 Test series defeat in South Africa. The knives were out. The BCCI were criticized for not attending to the game at grass-roots level; for anyone other than those involved in the national team, critics said, facilities for the players were poor. The ICL, Chandra said, could solve that problem and, ultimately, help nurture future Indian talent.

Notable former players – including Indian legend Kapil Dev, former England captain-turned-commentator Tony Grieg and Australia's Dean Jones – signed up to the initiative; several big-name players, such as Brian Lara and Shane Warne, were linked to it. In August 2007, the BCCI's response remained unequivocal. "Our stand is very clear," said Niranjan Shah, the board's secretary. "Players who take part in the ICL will never be eligible to play for the country [India] again." A week later, the board's president, Sharad Powar, went further. "Test cricket is the real thing. It is the top level of the game and brings out the best in players ...

Selling the game: Sachin Tendulkar – the most popular player in the world's most cricket-mad country – talks to the media at the launch of the Indian Premier League.

Twenty20 is for glamour. It can only bring in money." The comment could well have been set within the context of the hugely entertaining Test series being played out between England and India at the time (which India went on to win), but it was another well-directed slap in the face for the ICL.

A day later, the BCCI announced that any Indian player involved in the ICL would lose his benefits. Payments for domestic first-class players were increased. It was a classic "us or them" ultimatum. Later in the month, the BCCI announced plans to stage domestic Twenty20 leagues in four countries – India, Australia, South Africa and England. The ICL filed a petition against the BCCI to restrain them from "claiming to the public that they represent India". The International Cricket Council (ICC), the cricket world's governing body, refused to intervene in the domestic matter. National boards around the world followed suit, and advised their players not to take part in this unsanctioned event. A domestic inter-state tournament was held in India prior to the World Twenty20, for which the television rights remained pointedly unsold.

Before the start of proceedings in South Africa, the BCCI announced they would be launching an international Twenty20 competition from October 2008 featuring city-based teams, which would operate as franchises, and players from across the world. Present at the launch in Delhi were the three icons of Indian cricket, Sachin Tendulkar, Sourav Ganguly and Rahul Dravid, plus former New Zealand captain Stephen Fleming and the great Glenn McGrath. The presence of some of cricket's glitterati was a ringing endorsement for what would become the Indian Premier League (IPL). This was an officially sanctioned event, free to the best players in the world – although this would become a matter of future debate – and the concept had already started to capture the public's imagination.

In the end, with the odd exception (such as Shane Bond and Imran Farhat, who opted out of his central contract with Pakistan), those who signed for the ICL were either retired internationals (such as Brian Lara and Inzamam-ul-Haq) or those on the fringes of their national team (Chris Read and Darryl Tuffey). There was plenty of hype but, for the most part, the first edition of the breakaway tournament took place below the radar of the public's gaze. It seems certain the ICL will survive – four more tournaments were scheduled upon completion of the first – and continue to provide players' bank accounts with a significant cash boost, but the moment the BCCI opposed it, the ICL was unlikely ever to be a major player in the global game.

India's unexpected triumph at the World Twenty20 – and the fairy-tale manner in which it was achieved – simply accelerated the IPL's evolution. Prospective monies from the sale of television rights for a 20-over tournament spiralled upwards overnight. Forget October 2008, the demand for Twenty20 cricket in India was immediate. The IPL's player roster started to fill up – a list containing the names of more than 70 international cricketers. In January 2008, news emerged that Sony Enterprises had bagged the television rights for the IPL in a ten-year deal worth a staggering US$1 billion-plus – and 90 per cent of that money would pass to the BCCI. By

Who would have thought?: Rajasthan Royals, led by captain Shane Warne (right) were the inaugural Indian Premier League champions.

The Rise of the Indian Premier League

the end of January, the bidding process started for the eight franchises. The outcome of this raised more than a few eyebrows around the cricket world. The results of the franchise auction made the IPL a startling reality. The league's launch was brought forward to April. The eight city-based teams were named. Bidders came from areas previously unconnected with the game – India Cements, Bollywood, a Hyderabad-based newspaper and Mukesh Ambani, India's richest man – and the auction raised a colossal US$723.59 million, considerably higher than the base price of US$400 million. The IPL had become a blue-chip company in the blink of an eye. It merely added to the hype surrounding the impending player auction – and events at the Hilton Towers hotel on the Mumbai waterfront on 20 February 2008 certainly lived up to it.

You had to remind yourself it was cricket, not Hollywood. Team owners, supported by their icon players, arrived at the hotel. Players were presented in lots of six, with the marquee names the first to go under the hammer. The atmosphere was electric. Only ten players were sold during the auction's first two hours – at a mind-blowing value of US$7.175 million. India's Twenty20 captain Mahendra Singh Dhoni – the new pin-up boy of Indian cricket – went for US$1.5 million, one million more than his reserve price; Andrew Symonds – the man who had been at the centre of a race row during India's recent acrimonious tour of Australia – went for US$1.35 million. By the end of the evening, all but ten of the players – representing every Test-playing county bar England (whose board had refused to sanction the event) – had been contracted at a total cost of US$34.955 million.

The stage for the first edition of the Indian Premier League had been lavishly set. It would represent a landmark moment in cricket's distinguished history.

Most expensive player: Chennai Super Kings paid US$1.5 million to secure the services of MS Dhoni – the new pin-up boy of Indian cricket.

The Auction Process

The Franchises

Price (US$)	Franchise	Buyer
111.90m	Mumbai	Reliance India Ltd (Mukesh Ambani)
111.60m	Bangalore	UB Group (Vijay Mallya)
107.00m	Hyderabad	Deccan Chronicle
91.00m	Chennai	India Cements
84.00m	Delhi	GMR Group
76.00m	Mohali	Preity Zinta, Nesswadia, Karan Paul, Mohit Burman
75.09m	Kolkata	Red Chillies Entertainment (Shah Rukh Khan)
67.00m	Jaipur	Emerging Media-led consortium

The Leading Purchases at the IPL Auction

Player	Price	Franchise
Mahendra Singh Dhoni (Ind)	1,500,000	Chennai Super Kings
Andrew Symonds (Aus)	1,350,000	Deccan Chargers
Sachin Tendulkar (Ind)*	1,121,250	Mumbai Indians
Sourav Ganguly (Ind)*	1,092,500	Kolkata Knight Riders
Yuvraj Singh (Ind)*	1,063,750	Kings XI Punjab
Rahul Dravid (Ind)*	1,035,000	Bangalore Royal Challengers
Sanath Jayasuriya (SL)	975,000	Mumbai Indians
Ishant Sharma (Ind)	950,000	Kolkata Knight Riders
Irfan Pathan (Ind)	925,000	Kings XI Punjab
Jacques Kallis (SA)	900,000	Bangalore Royal Challengers
Brett Lee (Aus)	900,000	Kings XI Punjab
RP Singh (Ind)	875,000	Deccan Chargers
Harbhajan Singh (Ind)	850,000	Mumbai Indians
Virender Sehwag (Ind)*	833,750	Delhi Daredevils
Chris Gayle (WI)	800,000	Kolkata Knight Riders
Robin Uthappa (Ind)	800,000	Mumbai Indians
Rohit Sharma (Ind)	750,000	Deccan Chargers
Gautam Gambhir (Ind)	725,000	Delhi Daredevils
Adam Gilchrist (Aus)	700,000	Deccan Chargers
Brendon McCullum (NZ)	700,000	Kolkata Knight Riders
Kumar Sangakkara (SL)	700,000	Kings XI Punjab

* Designated icon player; not part of the player auction but receives 15 per cent more than franchise's highest-paid player

2008 Indian Premier League

The Indian Premier League had managed to lure a collection of the finest cricket-playing talent on the planet. Cricket had been taken to levels that were unheard of only months earlier. The stakes were high. The interest in the event had produced unprecedented hype. In short, the Indian Premier League had become the most talked-about event in the long and distinguished history of the game before a ball had been bowled. But the time for talk was over: 59 matches played out over a 45-day period would decide who would become the inaugural Indian Premier League champions.

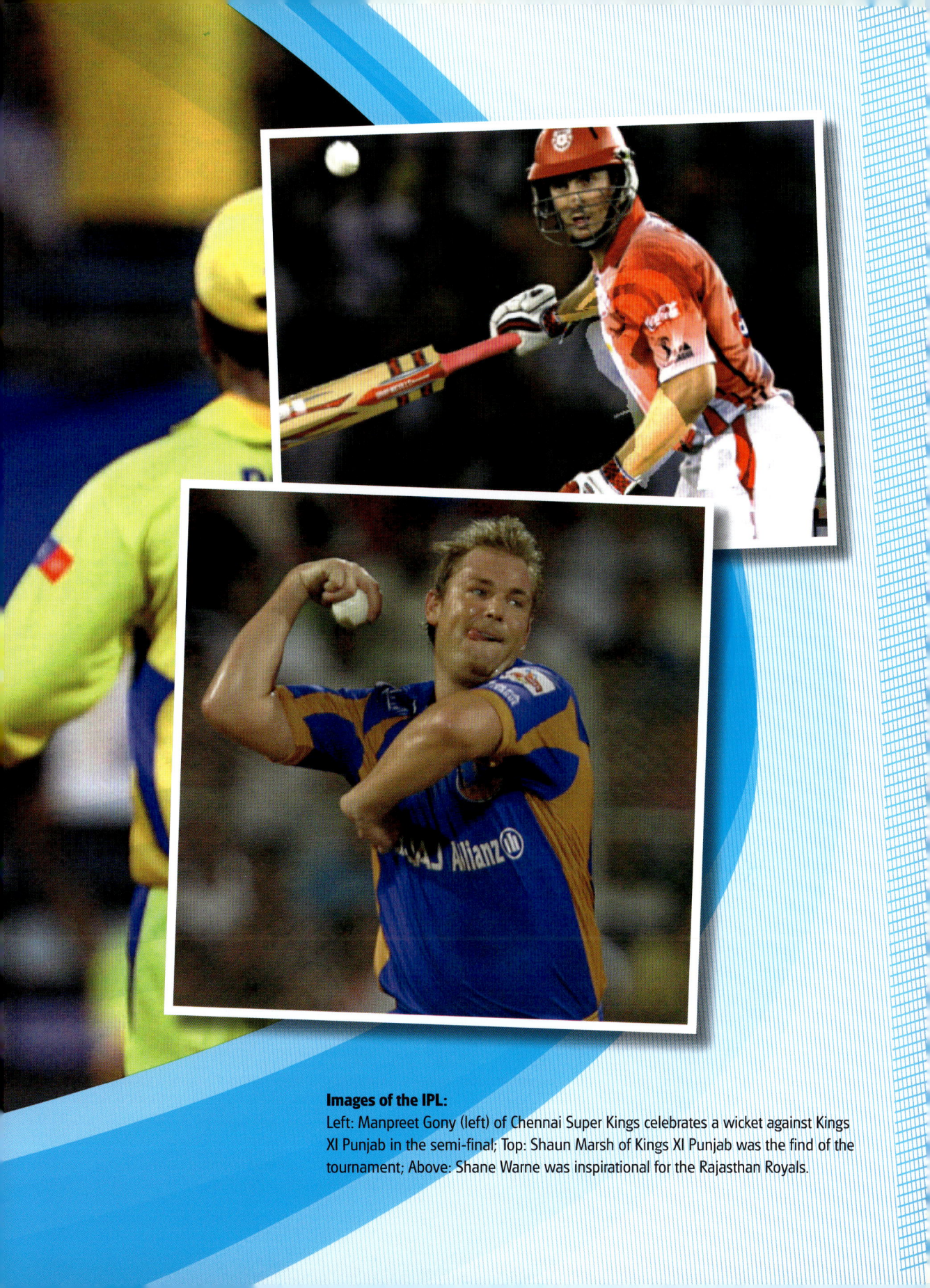

Images of the IPL:
Left: Manpreet Gony (left) of Chennai Super Kings celebrates a wicket against Kings XI Punjab in the semi-final; Top: Shaun Marsh of Kings XI Punjab was the find of the tournament; Above: Shane Warne was inspirational for the Rajasthan Royals.

Indian Premier League 2008 Review

After all the hype, the brazen multi-million-dollar exposure and a lavish opening ceremony more in keeping with the Olympic Games than a cricket tournament, the Indian Premier League finally got underway on 18 April 2008 with Bangalore playing host to Kolkata. And the Knight Riders' Brendon McCullum more than played his part in ensuring the 55,000-capacity crowd went home happy.

Bangalore's Chinnaswamy Stadium had witnessed pop stars belting out hits, stilt walkers, acrobats and a giant bubble, but the real fireworks started the moment Brendon McCullum strode to the crease. The New Zealand star was in mesmerizing form; unleashing a brutal assault on the Bangalore attack to swipe a Twenty20 record 158 not out, containing 13 sixes and ten fours, as the Knight Riders cruised to 222 for 3. Facing an asking rate of more than 11 runs per over, Bangalore did not stand a chance and limped meekly to 82 all out. It may not have been electricity all the way, but the organizers could not have hoped for a more explosive start.

The early rounds played out to the pre-tournament formbook. Mike Hussey hit a stylish unbeaten 116 as much-touted, heavy-spending Chennai beat Punjab by 33 runs. Elsewhere, Delhi crushed Rajasthan by nine wickets. The result left many feeling that Rajasthan, the cheapest franchise in the IPL, would pay the price for their sparse spending at the player auction, in which they were the only franchise to receive a fine for under-bidding.

But fortunes can change quickly in Twenty20 cricket ... and cricket followers have learned just how dangerous it is to write off Shane Warne. The legendary leg-spinner was captain of the Jaipur franchise – he was the only non-Indian player to lead a side in the IPL – and, putting aside his lacklustre display in the opening game, showed just what an inspirational figure he can be, leading from the front with the ball (taking 3 for 19) as the Royals restricted Punjab to 166 for 8. And where Warne led, fellow Australian Shane Watson was eager to follow. The injury-plagued all-rounder, using the IPL as a launchpad back into the Australian side, hit an unbeaten 76 to lead his side to a six-wicket victory. The Royals' shackles were off. Later in the week, Warne was at it again, smashing the Deccan Chargers' Andrew Symonds for two sixes in the final over to secure a memorable three-wicket win. And, in true underdog fashion, they continued to defy the critics, winning ten of their last 12 games to ease into the semi-finals.

The action on the field may have been newsworthy enough, but it was an off-the-field controversy that created the greatest number of newspaper column inches for the IPL. The Mumbai Indians, the tournament's most expensive franchise, hit by the absence through injury of their icon player, Sachin Tendulkar, had opened up with a five-wicket loss to Bangalore followed by a tense six-run loss to Chennai. Then came their match against Punjab. The 66-run defeat by Punjab pushed stand-in captain Harbhajan Singh over the edge. After the match, news emerged that Harbhajan had slapped his Indian team-mate Sreesanth. Pictures then flashed round the world showing the Indian pace bowler – himself notoriously never short of a word or two on a cricket pitch – walking around the ground in floods of tears. The media had a field day. It proved a costly lack of restraint by the Indian off-spinner: first he was suspended, then banned for the rest of the IPL season – but not before he and Sreesanth were made to embrace and make up before the television cameras. Mumbai's season, despite the best attentions of Shaun Pollock, veteran Sanath Jayasuriya and the late-returning Tendulkar, never recovered – they rallied towards the end of the campaign, but missed out on a semi-final spot in the final game.

Mumbai's was not the only tale of woe. The Deccan Chargers endured a miserable campaign, losing all but two of their 14 encounters. The Bangalore Royal Challengers, the IPL's second-most-expensive franchise, fared little better, winning just four of their games – with two of those victories coming in their last three fixtures, when the pressure was off. The major surprise was Kolkata's lacklustre showings. McCullum failed to reproduce the fireworks after his dynamic opening display; their captain and icon player Sourav Ganguly struggled; and Ricky Ponting – rattled by the paucity of his US$400,000 price tag – failed to produce the goods. The Knight Riders won six of their 14 games to finish in sixth place.

The success stories were equally captivating and none more so than the emergence of Western Australian Shaun Marsh. Better known before the start of the IPL as the son of former Australian opener Geoff, the 24-year-old left-hander proved the bargain buy of the tournament – snapped up by Kings XI Punjab for a paltry US$30,000. He also proved the batsman of the tournament, hitting six half-centuries in ten innings, with his crunching 115 not out against

Rajasthan in Punjab's final group game doing much to secure his side second spot in the table and a surprise place in the last four.

Delhi's made-in-India approach to team selection paid dividends. Relying on a core of Indian batsmen – led by icon player Virender Sehwag and World Twenty20 star Gautam Gambhir – and a largely foreign bowling attack (led by the ever-impressive Glenn McGrath), they overcame four straight defeats mid-campaign to take their place in the last four. They were joined by Chennai, who had opened with four straight wins, before slumping to three successive defeats following the departure of Matthew Hayden and Jacob Oram. Led by the inspirational Mahendra Singh Dhoni, who seemed to bring the best out of the Indian players left at his disposal, they rallied well.

SEMI-FINALS
Rajasthan's Shane Watson stamped his mark on the first semi-final in Mumbai. The Australian all-rounder – ably supported by Yusuf Pathan (45 off 21 balls) – produced a wonderful display of clean hitting during his 29-ball 52 to propel the Royals to an intimidating 192 for 9. He then produced a fiery opening spell with the ball (taking 3 for 10), removing danger-men Virender Sehwag and Gautam Gambhir as Delhi subsided to a disappointing 87 all out.

The second semi-final was another disappointingly one-sided affair. Punjab's batting, so solid throughout the tournament, came unstuck against some relentlessly accurate seam bowling from the Knight Riders. Muttiah Muralitharan may have been the surprise choice to open the attack, but it was the trio of Makhaya Ntini, Albie Morkel and MS Gony that did the damage, taking two wickets apiece as Punjab stumbled to 112 for 8. Chennai cruised past the total with a comfortable 31 balls to spare.

Semi-Final One
30 May 2008 at Mumbai
Rajasthan Royals 192 for 9 (20 overs) (SR Watson 52, MF Maharoof 3 for 34)
Delhi Daredevils 87 (16.1 overs) (SR Watson 3 for 10, MM Patel 3 for 17)
Rajasthan Royals won by 105 runs

Semi-Final Two
31 May 2008 at Mumbai
Kings XI Punjab 112 for 8 (20 overs)
Chennai Super Kings 116 for 1 (14.5 overs) (SK Raina 55*, PA Patel 51*)
Chennai Super Kings won by 9 wickets

FINAL
The pre-tournament favourites against the cheapest franchise in the league; the new golden boy of Indian cricket, Mahendra Singh Dhoni, pitting his wits against Shane Warne, the best captain Australia never had; a master screenwriter could not have conjured up a better finale. Chennai did well to post a challenging total of 163 for 3 on a two-paced Mumbai wicket. In reply, Rajasthan seemed to be wobbling on 42 for 3, before Shane Watson (28) and the impressive Yusuf Pathan (56) – who had earlier taken 3 for 22 – shared a stand of 65 quick-time runs to tip the match in the Royals' favour. A mini-collapse threatened to turn the tide, but with three wickets in hand, and eight runs required off the final over, captain Shane Warne and Sohail Tanvir – the tournament's leading wicket-taker – saw Rajasthan past the winning post off the final ball. It had been a sensational final and Rajasthan, the tournament's most consistent team, were fitting champions.

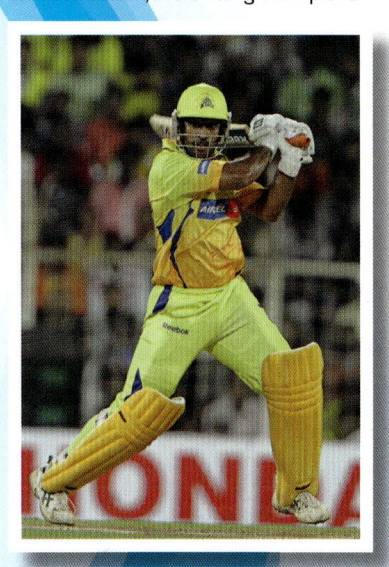

Worth his weight in gold: MS Dhoni scored more than 400 runs for Chennai on their way to the IPL Final.

Indian Premier League 2008: Final Table

Team	P	W	L	T	NR	Pts	NetRR	For	Against
Rajasthan	14	11	3	0	0	22	+0.632	2245/261.1	2153/270.2
Punjab	14	10	4	0	0	20	+0.509	2352/259.5	2271/265.5
Chennai	14	8	6	0	0	16	-0.192	2241/264.2	2195/253.1
Delhi	14	7	6	0	1	15	+0.342	2001/233.2	2031/246.4
Mumbai	14	7	7	0	0	14	+0.570	2080/249.1	2096/269.3
Kolkata	14	6	7	0	1	13	-0.147	1845/242.4	1718/221.4
Bangalore	14	4	10	0	0	8	-1.160	1983/272.4	2205/261.3
Deccan	14	2	12	0	0	4	-0.467	2229/270.0	2307/264.3

Indian Premier League 2008 Review

FINAL
1 June 2008
At Dr DY Patil Sports Academy, Mumbai
Rajasthan Royals beat Chennai Super Kings by 3 wickets

Chennai Super Kings

Batsman			R	B	4s	6s	SR
†PA Patel	c Kamran Akmal	b Pathan	38	33	5	0	115.15
S Vidyut	c Jadeja	b Pathan	16	14	1	1	114.28
SK Raina	c Jadeja	b Watson	43	30	1	2	143.33
JA Morkel	c Kamran Akmal	b Pathan	16	13	0	2	123.07
*MS Dhoni	not out		29	17	1	2	170.58
CK Kapugedera	c Asnodkar	b Sohail Tanvir	8	12	0	0	66.66
S Badrinath	not out		6	2	1	0	300.00
Extras	(b 1, lb 2, w 3, nb 1)		7				
Total	(5 wickets, 20 overs)		163				

Fall of wickets: 1-39, 2-64, 3-95, 4-128, 5-148
Did not bat: MS Gony, L Balaji, M Muralitharan, M Ntini
Bowling: Sohail Tanvir 4-0-40-1; Watson 4-0-29-1; Patel 2-0-14-0; Pathan 4-0-22-3; Trivedi 2-0-21-0; Warne 4-0-34-0

Rajasthan Royals

Batsman			R	B	4s	6s	SR
NK Patel		b Gony	2	11	0	0	18.18
SA Asnodkar	c Raina	b Morkel	28	20	4	0	140.00
†Kamran Akmal	run out	(Ntini)	6	7	1	0	85.71
SR Watson		b Muralitharan	28	19	3	0	147.36
YK Pathan	run out	(Raina)	56	39	3	4	143.58
M Kaif	c Dhoni	b Muralitharan	12	9	0	1	133.33
RA Jadeja	c Kapugedera	b Morkel	0	1	0	0	0.00
*SK Warne	not out		9	9	1	0	100.00
Sohail Tanvir	not out		9	7	0	0	128.57
Extras	(b 1, lb 6, w 5, nb 2)		14				
Total	(7 wickets, 20 overs)		164				

Fall of wickets: 1-19, 2-41, 3-42, 4-107, 5-139, 6-139, 7-143
Did not bat: SK Trivedi, MM Patel
Bowling: M Ntini 4-1-21-0; Gony 4-0-30-1; Morkel 4-0-25-2; Balaji 4-0-42-0; Muralitharan 4-0-39-2.

Umpires: BF Bowden (New Zealand) and RE Koertzen (South Africa)
Man of the Match: YK Pathan (Rajasthan Royals), *Player of the Series*: SR Watson (Rajasthan Royals)
Orange cap winner (awarded to batsman of the series): SE Marsh (Kings XI Punjab),
Purple cap winner (awarded to bowler of the series): Sohail Tanvir (Rajasthan Royals)

HONOURS BOARD 2008

Highest Total

Total	Team	Overs	RR	Inns	Opposition	Venue	Date
240/5	Chennai	20.0	12.00	1	Punjab	Mohali	19/04/2008

Biggest Margin of Victory – by runs

Margin	Winner	Target	Opposition	Venue	Date
140 runs	Kolkata	223	Bangalore	Bangalore	18/04/2008

By wickets

Margin	Winner	Balls Rem	Target	Overs	Opposition	Venue	Date
10 wkts	Deccan	48	155	12.0	Mumbai	Mumbai	27/04/2008

INDIVIDUAL HONOURS

Most Runs

Player	M	I	NO	Runs	HS	Ave	BF	SR	100	50
SE Marsh (Punjab)	11	11	2	616	115	68.44	441	139.68	1	5
G Gambhir (Delhi)	14	14	1	534	86	41.07	379	140.89	0	5
ST Jayasuriya (Mumbai)	14	14	2	514	114*	42.83	309	166.34	1	2
SR Watson (Rajasthan)	15	15	5	472	76*	47.20	311	151.76	0	4
GC Smith (Rajasthan)	11	11	2	441	91	49.00	362	121.82	0	3
AC Gilchrist (Deccan)	14	14	1	436	109*	33.53	318	137.10	1	3
YK Pathan (Rajasthan)	16	15	1	435	68	31.07	243	179.01	0	4
SK Raina (Chennai)	16	14	3	421	55*	38.27	298	142.71	0	3
MS Dhoni (Chennai)	16	14	4	414	65	41.40	310	133.54	0	2
V Sehwag (Delhi)	14	14	2	406	94*	33.83	220	184.54	0	3

Below: **Doing his bit:** Suresh Raina of Chennai Super Kings top-scored for his team in the final, took a catch and ran out Yusuf Pathan, but in a losing cause.

Above: **Super Shane:** The Indian Premier League player of the series was a blond Australian Shane W, but Watson not Warne.

Indian Premier League 2008 Review

Highest Score

Player	Runs	Balls	4s	6s	SR	Team	Opposition	Venue	Date
BB McCullum	158*	73	10	13	216.43	Kolkata	Bangalore	Bangalore	18/04/2008
A Symonds	117*	53	11	7	220.75	Deccan	Rajasthan	Hyderabad	24/04/2008
MEK Hussey	116*	54	8	9	214.81	Chennai	Punjab	Mohali	19/04/2008
SE Marsh	115	69	11	7	166.66	Punjab	Rajasthan	Mohali	28/05/2008
ST Jayasuriya	114*	48	9	11	237.50	Mumbai	Chennai	Mumbai	15/05/2008
AC Gilchrist	109*	47	9	10	231.91	Deccan	Mumbai	Mumbai	27/04/2008
V Sehwag	94*	41	10	6	229.26	Delhi	Deccan	Hyderabad	22/04/2008
KC Sangakkara	94	56	13	1	167.85	Punjab	Mumbai	Mohali	25/04/2008
SC Ganguly	91	57	11	5	159.64	Kolkata	Deccan	Hyderabad	11/05/2008
GC Smith	91	51	9	4	178.43	Rajasthan	Chennai	Chennai	24/05/2008

Most Wickets

Player	Mat	O	M	Runs	Wkts	BBI	Ave	Econ	SR	4w	5w
Sohail Tanvir (Rajasthan)	11	41.1	0	266	22	6/14	12.09	6.46	11.2	1	1
SK Warne (Rajasthan)	15	52.0	1	404	19	3/19	21.26	7.76	16.4	0	0
S Sreesanth (Punjab)	15	51.1	0	442	19	3/29	23.26	8.63	16.1	0	0
SR Watson (Rajasthan)	15	54.1	0	383	17	3/10	22.52	7.07	19.1	0	0
PP Chawla (Punjab)	15	46.5	0	389	17	3/25	22.88	8.30	16.5	0	0
JA Morkel (Chennai)	13	48.0	0	399	17	4/32	23.47	8.31	16.9	1	0
MS Gony (Chennai)	16	60.0	3	443	17	3/34	26.05	7.38	21.1	0	0
VY Mahesh (Delhi)	11	42.1	0	370	16	4/36	23.12	8.77	15.8	1	0
MF Maharoof (Delhi)	10	36.0	0	249	15	3/34	16.60	6.91	14.4	0	0
IK Pathan (Punjab)	14	53.0	2	350	15	2/18	23.33	6.60	21.2	0	0

Best Bowling in an Innings

Player	O	M	R	W	Econ	Team	Opposition	Venue	Date
Sohail Tanvir	4.0	0	14	6	3.50	Rajasthan	Chennai	Jaipur	04/05/2008
A Mishra	4.0	0	17	5	4.25	Delhi	Deccan	Delhi	15/05/2008
L Balaji	4.0	0	24	5	6.00	Chennai	Punjab	Chennai	10/05/2008
Shoaib Akhtar	3.0	0	11	4	3.66	Kolkata	Delhi	Kolkata	13/05/2008
Sohail Tanvir	4.0	0	14	4	3.50	Rajasthan	Mumbai	Jaipur	26/05/2008
CRD Fernando	4.0	0	18	4	4.50	Mumbai	Bangalore	Bangalore	28/05/2008
M Ntini	4.0	0	21	4	5.25	Chennai	Kolkata	Kolkata	18/05/2008
Umar Gul	4.0	0	23	4	5.75	Kolkata	Punjab	Kolkata	25/05/2008
GD McGrath	4.0	0	29	4	7.25	Delhi	Bangalore	Delhi	30/04/2008
JA Morkel	4.0	0	32	4	8.00	Chennai	Bangalore	Chennai	21/05/2008

Most Sixes

Player	No. of innings	No. of sixes
ST Jayasuriya (Mumbai)	14	31
SE Marsh (Punjab)	11	26
YK Pathan (Rajasthan)	15	25
V Sehwag (Delhi)	14	21
RG Sharma (Deccan)	12	19
AC Gilchrist (Deccan)	14	19
Yuvraj Singh (Punjab)	14	19
SR Watson (Rajasthan)	15	19
SK Raina (Chennai)	14	18
DJ Hussey (Kolkata)	13	17

Best Economy Rate (qualification 4 wickets)

Player	O	M	R	W	Best	Ave	Econ	4w	5w
SC Ganguly (Kolkata)	20.0	0	128	6	2/21	21.33	6.40	0	0
Sohail Tanvir (Rajasthan)	41.1	0	233	22	6/14	12.09	6.46	1	1
SM Pollock (Mumbai)	46.0	1	301	11	3/12	27.36	6.54	0	0
IK Pathan (Punjab)	53.0	2	350	15	2/18	23.33	6.60	0	0
GD McGrath (Delhi)	54.0	2	357	12	4/29	29.75	6.61	1	0
DW Steyn (Bangalore)	38.0	0	252	10	3/27	25.20	6.63	0	0
AB Dinda (Kolkata)	39.0	0	260	9	3/33	28.88	6.66	0	0
A Mishra (Delhi)	20.0	0	138	11	5/17	12.54	6.90	0	1
M Ntini (Chennai)	35.0	2	242	7	4/21	34.57	6.91	1	0
MF Maharoof (Delhi)	36.0	0	249	15	3/34	16.60	6.91	0	0

Orange Cap: A snip at US$30,000, Western Australian Shaun Marsh – the son of former Aussie opener Geoff Marsh – was the surprise star of the inaugural Indian Premier League, amassing 616 runs at the impressive average of 68.44.

2008 Indian Premier League Team of the Year

1. Shaun Marsh* (Kings)
616 runs (ave: 68.44; scoring rate: 139.68)
Shaun Marsh was the find of the tournament. The left-hander, son of former Australian opener Geoff, missed the first four games of the IPL but hit the ground running. He hit six half-centuries, including a match-winning 115 not out against eventual champions Rajasthan in the group stages, en route to ending as the tournament's leading run-scorer with 616 runs. His performances earned him a call-up to Australia's Twenty20 side against the West Indies in June 2008 and a place in the Test squad.

2. Gautam Gambhir (Delhi)
534 runs (ave: 41.07; scoring rate: 140.89)
Gautam Gambhir continued the good form he had shown during India's successful march to the World Twenty20 crown in South Africa with some eye-catching performances at the top of the Delhi order. The spearhead of the Daredevils' made-in-India batting philosophy, he prospered in the role, hitting five half-centuries, with a top score of 86 coming against Bangalore. He was the first batsman in the competition to pass the 400-run milestone.

3. Suresh Raina (Chennai)
421 runs (ave: 38.27; scoring rate: 142.71)
Regular contributions from the swashbuckling Suresh Raina did much to help Chennai overcome the cruel early loss of run-laden Matthew Hayden and forge a path to the competition's final stages. Though he has struggled to establish himself in the national side, the 21-year-old's performances in the IPL did much to force his way back into the international reckoning, with his assured unbeaten 55 in the semi-final particularly catching the eye.

4. Shane Watson* (Rajasthan)
472 runs (ave: 47.20; scoring rate: 151.76); 17 wickets (ave: 22.52; economy: 7.07)
Shane Watson's blistering performances for the Rajasthan Royals at last saw him live up to his long-time billing as Australia's next great all-rounder. Finally putting his injury nightmare behind him, the Queenslander was consistently destructive with the bat (finishing as the tournament's fourth-highest run-scorer with 472 runs) and both effective and aggressive with the ball (he was the fourth-highest wicket-taker, with 17 wickets). He was the unanimous choice for Player of the Tournament.

5. Yusuf Pathan (Rajasthan)
435 runs (ave: 31.07; scoring rate: 179.01); 8 wickets (ave: 28.75; economy: 8.16)
Yusuf Pathan's violent approach to batting blossomed under the leadership of Shane Warne and evolved into a weapon of match-winning capability. Of all the batsmen in the competition to score more than 200 runs, only Virender Sehwag scored them more quickly, and Pathan's match-winning contribution in

Hard hat area: Yusuf Pathan of Rajasthan Royals displayed an uncomplicated and spectacular batting style, scoring at almost 180 runs per hundred balls.

the final did much to drag the 25-year-old out of the shadow cast over his career by the success of his World Twenty20-winning half-brother Irfan. He also made some miserly contributions with the ball.

6. Mahendra Singh Dhoni (Chennai, wicketkeeper)
414 runs (ave: 41.40; scoring rate: 133.54)
It was always going to be hard for Mahendra Singh Dhoni to live up to his ludicrously inflated US$1.5 million auction tag, but the new glamour boy of Indian cricket made the best of a difficult job. Tidy behind the stumps and as innovative as ever as captain, he also made some major contributions to the Super Kings' cause with the bat, hitting 414 runs – of the wicketkeepers, only Adam Gilchrist (436) scored more – at a healthy average of 41.40.

7. Rohit Sharma (Deccan)
404 runs (ave: 36.72; scoring rate: 147.98)
Bought for a staggering US$750,000 off the back of some encouraging performances for India during the World Twenty20 in South Africa, Rohit Sharma was one of the few leading lights for the Deccan Chargers in what was otherwise a miserable campaign for the Hyderabad franchise. The 21-year-old showed the classical approach can be an effective one in the 20-over game, with his lofted drives and vicious cuts seeing him amass a more than respectable 404 runs in a struggling side.

8. Sohail Tanvir* (Rajasthan)
36 runs (ave: 12.00; scoring rate: 124.13); 22 wickets (ave: 12.09; economy: 6.46)
The best bowler on show during the 2008 Indian Premier League season, Sohail Tanvir's hard-to-read action and devilish mixture of slower balls and yorkers took him to a competition-leading haul of 22 wickets (at an average of 12.09) while conceding fewer than seven runs per over. The Pakistan paceman also showed he was no mug with the bat, and was used as a pinch-hitter on occasion by Rajasthan captain Shane Warne.

9. Shane Warne* (Rajasthan, captain)
70 runs (ave: 14.00; scoring rate: 118.64); 19 wickets (ave: 21.26; economy: 7.76)
Shane Warne's fast-thinking, innovative approach to captaincy was always likely to make him seem an inspired choice as Rajasthan's captain, but no one could have predicted the impact he made on the IPL's cheapest franchise. The Australian inspired both the Indian players and overseas stars alike, galvanizing the team into a fearsome, consistent and ultimately competition-winning unit. He showed he still had what it takes with the ball, too; his haul of 19 wickets was the second-highest in the competition.

10. Manpreet Gony (Chennai)
35 runs (ave: 35.00; scoring rate: 152.17); 17 wickets (ave: 26.05; economy: 7.38)
Along with the US$30,000 spent on Shaun Marsh, the US$50,000 splashed out on Manpreet Gony represented the best value-for-money transaction of the 2008 Indian Premier League. The tall medium-pacer made the most of Chennai's policy of relying on Indian bowlers and led from the front, taking 17 wickets – the fourth-largest haul of the tournament. His performances for the Super Kings earned him a call-up to the Indian one-day international side.

11. S Sreesanth (Punjab)
19 wickets (ave: 23.26; economy: 8.63)
He may have captured the headlines for all the wrong reasons in the early weeks of the competition, but Sreesanth put his unfortunate altercation with Harbhajan Singh behind him and used the remainder of the Indian Premier League season to show he was India's leading strike bowler in the 20-over format of the game. He was a touch expensive (going for over eight runs an over), but only Sohail Tanvir bettered his tournament haul of 19 wickets.

* one of four permitted overseas players

Captain Fantastic: Astute leadership and canny bowling saw Shane Warne stamp his mark on the inaugural Indian Premier League season.

Sir Allen Stanford – The US$20 Million-Dollar Game

Sir Allen Stanford was never going to remain on the fringes of world cricket for long. Having built his own state-of-the-art stadium in Antigua, ploughed money into West Indian domestic cricket and staged his own fully sanctioned domestic Twenty20 tournament, all that remained for the Texan billionaire was to attract matches with an international pedigree.

He chose the build-up to the World Twenty20 in South Africa in September 2007 – a time when the cricket world's attention was firmly focused on the 20-over game – to announce he was on the verge of signing a five-year deal to stage the Stanford 20/20 with the West Indies Cricket Board (WICB). It was a win-win announcement for both parties: the first tournament – in 2005–06 – had been held to great acclaim, the format had proved popular with the punters (and television rights had been sold accordingly) and, as part of the deal, Stanford had poured money into the cash-starved West Indian cricket infrastructure. As business decisions went for both parties, it was a no-brainer.

But the timing was more than prescient. It was Stanford saying to the cricket world that his ultimate ambitions had a broader perspective and, a day after India's last-gasp win over Pakistan in the World Twenty20 final in Johannesburg, he invited the newly crowned champions to play in a one-off, winner-takes-all, US$5 million match at his ground in Antigua in June 2008. An official invitation was sent through the WICB; Stanford claimed he had Australia as backup. The Board of Control for Cricket in India (BCCI) said they were unwilling to allow their team to play in a "private" event; the Australians remained silent; and the match ultimately came to nought.

Even this had been a compromise. Stanford's original intention had been

They'll be choking on their sandwiches in the Pavilion: Sir Allen Stanford dropped in to visit Lord's in unconventional style, but when you are putting in US$20 million for a single game, you can do just about anything!

to stage a quadrangular tournament between Australia, India, South Africa and Sri Lanka. The winners would then take on the Stanford Superstars – a team of players made up from those who had appeared in the Stanford 20/20 – for a winner's prize of US$20 million. He invited the respective boards to a meeting, while they were all in South Africa. "I called it 20/20 for 20," mused the Texan. None of the boards showed for the meeting. Reports suggested Stanford's relationship with the ICC was strained. Stanford was not to know it at the time, but the BCCI had bigger plans for their Twenty20 players – they were busy organizing their own private event.

The second edition of the Stanford 20/20 took place in January and February 2008. Once again it was a great hit with the locals, as Trinidad and Tobago walked away with the million-dollar prize money after crushing Jamaica by nine wickets in the final. For the most part, however, the event had passed beyond the gaze of the wider cricket public. By this time, the Indian Premier League was the talk of the cricketing town. No sooner had Stanford's own domestic tournament come to a conclusion, however, than further announcements were made. This time the Texan mooted plans to stage a winner-takes-all showdown for a staggering US$20 million and Australia and England were the targets.

"It's what I call the OK Corral. Anytime, anyplace, you come to our field and play one game ... You get England or Australia to come down and play our little eight or nine million population collective group of islands. Let me take our best players from those islands and play you right here for US$20 million and we'll see who wins." It all sounded like a verbal onslaught from a pumped-up television preacher, but the words contained plenty of temptation.

The rise of the IPL had left many of world cricket's national boards floundering. The moment the ICC sanctioned the event the floodgates opened and players signed up in droves – those with no scheduled international commitments and primarily those from lesser-funded boards. Every one of the respective boards gave their players permission to play, albeit reluctantly, knowing they had little choice in the matter. There was one exception: England.

The England and Wales Cricket Board (ECB) had been against the IPL from the word go – mainly because it clashed with the start of the domestic season in England and the arrival of a touring side from New Zealand. They had forbidden their players to play in the event and the BCCI had agreed not to approach them – although England's talisman all-rounder Andrew Flintoff said he had received an approach. But this was not a status quo that could last for ever. England's players had openly expressed their desire to play in the IPL at a future stage – in addition to fulfilling their international commitments – and there was little doubt the IPL would be very glad to have them. The ECB must have thought Stanford's proposal offered the glimmer of a long-term solution.

Here was a man who, like them, wanted to stand up to the BCCI and the IPL. And here was a man who, unlike them, had the financial clout to compete with them. Some may have questioned Allen Stanford's true intentions – the popular argument being that all Stanford wanted was to fund the rise of Twenty20 to the point where it cracked the US market (and the real money) and damn the effect on the game of cricket – but the ECB appeared more than happy to go along for the moment. As far as they were concerned, the cash on offer was the ideal sweetener to appease the players. The international fixture list also worked very much in their favour.

It took weeks of discussion – and a helicopter visit to cricket's fabled headquarters by Stanford – before a deal was struck. England would play the Stanford Superstars once a year for the next five years – with a jackpot of US$20 million on offer to the winning team each year. It was a deal that could secure a player's future – provided they won the match. All of a sudden, county players across England had even more reason to take Twenty20 cricket more seriously. And the competition for places on the plane to Antigua on 1 November 2008 started with the Twenty20 Cup.

Doing it his way: Sir Allen Stanford has the money to take on the BCCI.

Stanford 20/20 for US$20 million

Rarely has a game of cricket prompted as much hype and debate. After months of talk, and following a last-minute legal wrangle over who held the rights for the match (and what share of the huge financial pie various parties were entitled to), England's players flew out to Antigua for potentially the most fiscally rewarding week of their careers.

When the ECB signed up with Allen Stanford to play five matches over five years against a West Indies select XI at the Texan billionaire's cricket ground, it provoked a torrent of vitriol from the game's traditionalists. This was the ECB's public refusal to kowtow to the BCCI's unprecedented grip on the world game; this was seen as a means of compensating, and retaining control of, the England players after they had been barred from playing in the Indian Premier League. But it was a crass use of brand England: cricket should be about the honour of playing for your country, about the need to defend national pride, and not about bolstering the coffers of the ECB and, potentially, the pockets of its players. When the action finally got underway, the voices of the many dissenters simply increased in volume.

The two victorious warm-up matches (England beat Trinidad and Tobago and English champions Middlesex) raised questions about the standard of the wicket, the quality of the lights, and the behaviour of Sir Allen Stanford himself, after the Texan was seen cavorting in the crowd, with the wife of one of the England players on his knee, and was reported to have walked in and out of the dressing rooms as though he owned the place – which, of course, he did. As the tension mounted, and food poisoning started to run riot throughout the England camp, their captain, Kevin Pietersen, announced that, for him, the week could not end quickly enough.

It turned out to be one of most one-sided matches in international Twenty20 cricket's short history. The match was as good as over at the halfway stage: a dismal England fell for an abject 99 all out, with only two of their batsmen

Triumph and Dejection: England captain Kevin Pietersen, left, muses on what might have been while Stanford Superstars skipper Daren Powell admires the trophy.

50 Stanford 20/20 for US $20 million

(Samit Patel and Paul Collingwood) reaching double figures. The Stanford Superstars, led by the excellent Chris Gayle (65 not out), dashed past England's total in just 12.4 overs.

As the West Indian players celebrated their biggest payday and fireworks spilled out over the Antiguan sky, the ramifications of England's poor performance started to sink in. This had been a poor advert for international cricket by any standard. What's more, the problems the match was supposed to solve (financial compensation for players) loomed as large as ever. It seems inevitable that England's players will travel en masse to compete in the IPL in the near future and the ECB, through nothing more than a desire to retain a sense of power in the world game, are left with a match that, in international terms at least, can be seen as little more than a white elephant.

The second edition of the Stanford 20/20 will take place in November 2009: that the ECB have already intimated that it might be an ECB XI — as opposed to an England XI — that takes to the pitch, tells you all you need to know. The first edition of the most-talked-about series of matches in cricket's history may already be over, but the jury is still very much out on whether Allen Stanford and his seemingly limitless amounts of cash can bring any real value to this most traditional of games.

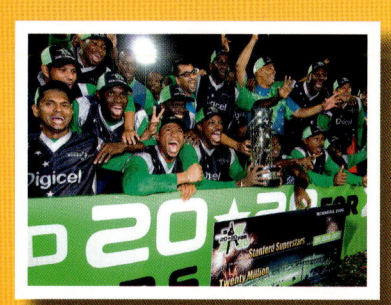

Stanford Superstars v England
1 November 2008 at Stanford Cricket Ground, Coolidge, Antigua

England

Batsman			R	M	B	4s	6s	SR
IR Bell		b Taylor	7	16	11	0	0	63.63
†MJ Prior		b Taylor	12	18	11	2	0	109.09
OA Shah	c Mohammed	b Sammy	4	10	8	0	0	50.00
*KP Pietersen		b Sammy	7	17	14	0	0	50.00
A Flintoff		b Pollard	8	24	12	1	0	66.66
PD Collingwood	c Sarwan	b Benn	10	18	15	1	0	66.66
SR Patel	run out		22	29	24	2	0	91.66
LJ Wright	c Sammy	b Pollard	1	4	5	0	0	20.00
GP Swann		b Benn	3	3	3	0	0	100.00
SCJ Broad	not out		9	24	12	0	0	75.00
SJ Harmison		b Benn	6	4	4	1	0	150.00
Extras	(lb 1, w 9)		10					
Total	(all out, 19.5 overs)		99					

Fall of wickets: 1-21, 2-22, 3-29, 4-33, 5-51, 6-54, 7-59, 8-63, 9-92, 10-99

Bowling	O	M	R	W	Econ
DJG Sammy	4.0	0	13	2	3.25
JE Taylor	4.0	0	25	2	6.25
DBL Powell	4.0	0	18	0	4.50
SJ Benn	3.5	0	16	3	4.17
KA Pollard	4.0	0	26	2	6.50

Stanford Superstars

Batsman		R	M	B	4s	6s	SR
*CH Gayle	not out	65	58	45	5	5	144.44
†ADS Fletcher	not out	32	58	31	5	0	103.22
Extras	(lb 1, w 3)	4					
Total	(0 wickets 12.4 overs)	101					

Did not bat: RR Sarwan, S Chanderpaul, SC Joseph, KA Pollard, DJG Sammy, SJ Benn, D Mohammed, JE Taylor, DBL Powell

Bowling	O	M	R	W	Econ
SJ Harmison	3.0	0	30	0	10.00
SCJ Broad	3.0	0	24	0	8.00
A Flintoff	3.4	0	25	0	6.81
SR Patel	1.0	0	9	0	9.00
PD Collingwood	1.0	0	4	0	4.00
GP Swann	1.0	0	8	0	8.00

Stanford Superstars won by 10 wickets
Man of the Match: DJG Sammy

Twenty million reasons to celebrate: The members of the Stanford Superstars are all smiles after each of the starting XI collected US$1million for beating England by ten wickets in the special challenge match in Antigua.

The Twenty20 Cup 2008

The Indian Premier League had switched the world's gaze to 20-over cricket. As a result, the build-up to the Twenty20 Cup in England – the competition that started the new global sporting fad – received far more attention than had been the case in previous years. Not that anyone thought the competition could realistically rival the IPL; it was just proof, if more were needed, that the cricket public had embraced 20-over cricket; and everyone knew that, this time round, with Champions League riches on offer to the winning team, there was more at stake in the competition than ever. Fortunately, the 2008 Twenty20 Cup merely enhanced 20-over cricket's ever-growing reputation.

Twenty20 visions:
Left: **Packed houses:** The English public's love affair with the Twenty20 Cup continued in 2008.
Top: **Joe Denly:** A consistent producer at the top of the order for the Kent Spitfires.
Above: **Middlesex Crusaders:** The most consistent side in the 2008 competition and worthy winners.

To Play or Not to Play: The Ultimate Question

In hindsight, the international cricket calendar that had worked to the English game's advantage for so many years – the majority of the domestic season does not overlap that of any other Test-playing country – always had the potential to work against it. And when the Board of Control for Cricket in India (BCCI) decided to launch the Indian Premier League in April 2008, coinciding with the start of the English domestic season, it left the England and Wales Cricket Board (ECB), English cricket's governing body, with little room for manoeuvre.

The ECB could not afford to lose its best players to the lure of the Indian rupee and to a tournament that cut a swathe through the early part of the English season. The international cricket calendar dictates that the early season tour to England is one of the few, if not the only, Test series being played out anywhere in the world – and the amount the ECB receives in television rights for this exclusive Test series rises proportionately. The ECB needed its best players on the park at Lord's or The Oval, and not plying their trade in Mumbai or Kolkata. What's more, with the English domestic game already on its knees in terms of spectator numbers – with the exception of the Twenty20 Cup – it could ill afford to lose its leading lights for the best part of two months. Not that this was the line the ECB gave to the media.

"We don't want them turning up exhausted. The spectators of this country want to know that our players are as fit and as sharp and ready for the Australia series [in 2009] as we can ensure that they are," said ECB chairman Giles Clark, in deference to the fact that a six-week stint in the IPL playing 20-over cricket would provide scant preparation for a tough Ashes campaign. It is a flimsy argument – there are, after all, plenty of Australians playing in the IPL – and it has done little to slow down their victorious march through world cricket. The real argument was about who had control of the players.

The IPL had placed the English domestic season in considerable jeopardy. The ECB's response to it was to bar its centrally contracted players from appearing in the tournament. In the end, Hampshire's Dimitri Mascarenhas (who was not contracted by the ECB and, therefore, did not need its permission to play) was the only English player to experience the razzmatazz of cricket's most exciting event.

The deal struck between the ECB and Allen Stanford could well placate the players for now, but it can only be a short-term fix for what is sure to become a long-term problem. The players will want to be able to make a choice.

A sense of the inevitable hovers over the English game. The IPL has already made approaches to England's

Saying "no" for now: Andrew Flintoff admitted to having been approached by the Indian Premier League, and it seems only a matter of time before he appears in it.

talisman all-rounder Andrew Flintoff; Kevin Pietersen, the side's captain and star batsman, has expressed an interest in appearing in the tournament. There may be trouble ahead: the Professional Cricketers' Association (PCA), charged with looking after the players' best interests, certainly thought so, and lashed out at the ECB, predicting a possible players' revolt.

"It is human nature that they [the players] want to play in the IPL," said PCA chief executive Sean Morris. "You can't fight the market. The cricket market has had a significant amount of money going into it and we should be looking to capitalize on it and develop it, not be King Canute."

The ECB's response was that players would not dream of jeopardizing their central contracts for six weeks of cricket. There are two problems with that argument. Firstly, the cricket world is a small one; if players from Australia, South Africa and New Zealand, to name but three, are playing in the IPL and revelling in its super-charged atmosphere, word of it will sweep around the dressing rooms – players dream of performing in such an environment. And then there was the issue of money – could the ECB adequately compensate their players for not appearing in the IPL and, if so, for how long?

"If you are trying to prevent people from migrating for the money, that is not going to work because, ultimately, money talks – and there is an awful lot of it in the IPL ... The players are very excited by it," continued Morris.

"If you're going to restrict players contractually, the issue comes up because the opportunity is so great. Players will begin to look at their contracts and feel that they would want more flexibility. There is a wealth of talent out there and quite understandably the value of the cricketer has increased significantly through what is happening in the IPL. It is perfectly natural for any cricketer and for the PCA to want our members to take advantage of that – it is a truly unique opportunity."

The ECB's Stanford solution will only work if England's players win all five of their annual contests against the Texan billionaire's Superstars – and that is far from guaranteed. In addition, how many members of the England squad will be around for all five editions of the series? Talk of a player rebellion might be a little far-fetched, but it is not inconceivable that the money on offer in the IPL will have a huge impact on a number of players' career plans. Why plough a furrow through a congested international calendar – particularly if you are an injury-prone bowler – when you can receive a similar sum of cash for six weeks' work in the IPL? If you are a leading county player, constantly on the edge of national selectors' thoughts, which would be the better alternative? The ECB has done little to find an answer to these questions, and it will have to come up with a solution ... and fast.

This was the debate raging in the weeks prior to the start of the 2008 Twenty20 Cup, and its resolution will have far-reaching consequences for the long-term future of the game.

Missing out: England captain Kevin Pietersen has openly admitted his desire to experience the razzmatazz of the Indian Premier League.

The Twenty20 Cup 2008 Review

Following the success of the Indian Premier League and the added lure of a US$5 million prize-fund for the two Champions League qualifiers, not to mention the possibility of securing a place in England's Twenty20 team and a shot at Sir Allen Stanford's millions, the stakes had never been so high in the Twenty20 Cup.

North Division
Back-to-back victories over Derbyshire set Durham's Twenty20 campaign ball rolling and they went on to suffer only a single defeat, against Nottinghamshire, en route to the quarter-finals. Lancashire's campaign could well have been derailed following a loss to Durham and the ignominy of home-and-away defeats to cross-Pennine arch-rivals Yorkshire but, led by Kolpak signing François du Plessis (57 v Nottinghamshire) and overseas player Lou Vincent (an unbeaten 102 against Derbyshire), they rallied well to secure the final automatic qualification berth. Yorkshire overcame two opening defeats by winning four games on the bounce, but it still took a final-game nine-wicket win over Nottinghamshire to secure one of the two quarter-final best-losers' slots. It was a Twenty20 season to forget, however, for both Derbyshire (three wins) and two-time champions Leicestershire (two wins).

Mid/Wales/West Division
Warwickshire and Northamptonshire were the form sides of the Mid/Wales/West Division. The Bears recorded a sequence of six wins en route to their place at the top of the group table, with 19-year-old Chris Woakes (4 for 21 v Somerset) and Jonathan Trott (61 not out v Worcestershire and an unbeaten half-century against Gloucestershire) catching the eye. Andrew Hall's early-season heroics with bat and ball propelled Northamptonshire to the top of the group table, and they confirmed their status as surprise package of the tournament by churning out the wins and maintaining their grip on the second qualification berth. Glamorgan, Gloucestershire and Somerset were left to rue the unpredictable West Country weather, recording ten no-results between them. Somerset batsman Marcus Trescothick made the most of the sun when it did shine, however, hitting a swashbuckling – and eye-catching – 57-ball 107 against Worcestershire. A paltry three wins from ten games was a poor return for the New Road outfit.

South Division
Four half-centuries, including a 57-ball 91, in the first seven matches by 22-year-old opener Joe Denly provided the ballast for defending champion Kent's faltering attempt to hang on to their trophy, with a final-match victory over Sussex enough to deny Hampshire a place in the quarter-finals via the final best-losers' slot. The form team of the division was Middlesex, whose eight wins, including a season-opening five in a row, were enough to see them to top spot. Essex, aided by some mesmeric performances from Graham Napier (including an innings of 152 against Sussex that included a world-record 16 sixes), recovered from two defeats in their opening three matches to secure the second qualification berth. A crushing final-match defeat to Essex left Hampshire wondering what could have been, but for Surrey and Sussex – both of whom had the misfortune to suffer sequences of five straight defeats – the 2009 Twenty20 Cup, and a chance for redemption, cannot come quickly enough.

Quarter-finals
There was controversy at Chester-le-Street just moments before the start of the first quarter-final between Durham and Yorkshire. News emerged from the ECB that Yorkshire had fielded an ineligible player in their final group match against Nottinghamshire. The

Take that: Lancashire's Kolpak signing François du Plessis showed great promise.

player in question was Azeem Rafiq, a 17-year-old former England U15 and U17 player (and captain) who had not been registered to play in the competition and who, it later emerged, did not hold a British passport. Rafiq took 0 for 18 off his two overs in that match; Yorkshire were thrown out of the competition; Glamorgan took their place in the quarter-finals. As administrative errors go, rarely could there have been a more expensive one. Glamorgan's reprieve was short-lived, however. They ended up losing the hastily rearranged quarter-final to Durham by 44 runs.

Elsewhere, Ravi Bopara (47) and Graham Napier (4 for 10) helped Essex to a 59-run victory over Northamptonshire. At The Oval, Middlesex – playing at their temporary home while England hosted South Africa in the first Test at Lord's – brushed aside a Lancashire XI containing six internationals to take their place in the final four. Andrew Flintoff, fresh on the comeback trail following more trouble with his suspect ankle, impressed with both bat and ball (53 and 3 for 17), but the star of the show was Middlesex's 20-year-old, South African-born left-hander, Dawid Malan, whose 54-ball 103 led Middlesex to a testing total of 176 for 7 and left Lancashire chasing the game. The visitors ultimately fell 12 runs short.

In the fourth of the scheduled quarter-finals, champions Kent kept alive their hopes of becoming the first team to defend the trophy with a comprehensive 42-run win over Warwickshire at Edgbaston, with Darren Stevens (69) and Yasir Arafat (3 for 29) the star performers.

The scene was now set for 26 July and finals day at Hampshire's Rose Bowl. The rise in temperature was palpable.

North Division

Team	P	W	L	T	NR	Pts	NetRR	For	Against
Durham (Q)	10	6	1	1	2	15	+0.984	1013/122.4	982/135.0
Lancashire (Q)	10	6	3	0	1	13	+0.921	1361/171.4	1252/178.4
Yorkshire (Q)	10	5	3	1	1	10	-0.312	1236/162.4	1300/164.2
Nottinghamshire	10	4	5	0	1	9	+0.027	1264/170.3	1273/172.2
Derbyshire	10	3	7	0	0	6	-0.421	1280/183.0	1268/171.0
Leicestershire	10	2	7	0	1	5	-0.893	1197/180.0	1276/169.1

Midlands/West/Wales Division

Team	P	W	L	T	NR	Pts	NetRR	For	Against
Warwickshire (Q)	10	6	1	1	2	15	+0.694	1126/150.3	1086/160.0
Northants (Q)	10	6	3	0	1	13	+0.431	1469/175.2	1363/171.3
Glamorgan*	10	3	3	0	4	10	-0.176	952/115.5	971/115.4
Somerset	10	3	4	0	3	9	+0.313	1209/140.0	1161/139.3
Worcestershire	10	3	6	0	1	7	-0.488	1339/176.5	1428/177.1
Gloucestershire	10	1	5	1	3	6	-0.931	990/138.4	1076/133.2

South Division

Team	P	W	L	T	NR	Pts	NetRR	For	Against
Middlesex (Q)	10	8	2	0	0	16	+0.732	1414/177.3	1358/188.0
Essex (Q)	10	6	3	1	0	13	+0.937	1519/192.0	1346/193.0
Kent (Q)	10	6	4	0	0	12	+0.640	1563/187.5	1444/188.0
Hampshire	10	5	4	1	0	11	-0.505	1536/197.1	1572/189.3
Sussex	10	2	8	0	0	4	-0.876	1394/186.5	1616/193.5
Surrey	10	2	8	0	0	4	-0.905	1462/198.0	1550/187.0

* Glamorgan awarded place in quarter-finals after Yorkshire were thrown out of the competition for fielding an unregistered player

The Twenty20 Cup 2008

Quarter-finals

at Chester-le-Street, 7 July 2008
Durham v Yorkshire
Match cancelled without a ball being bowled (*)

at Chelmsford, 7 July 2008
Essex 192 for 9 (20 overs) (RS Bopara 47)
Northamptonshire 115 for 7 (18 overs) (GR Napier 4 for 10) (Target: 175 from 18 overs)
Essex beat Northamptonshire by 59 runs (D/L Method)

at The Oval, 8 July 2008
Middlesex 176 for 7 (20 overs) (DJ Malan 103, A Flintoff 3 for 17)
Lancashire 164 for 8 (20 overs) (A Flintoff 53)
Middlesex beat Lancashire by 12 runs

at Edgbaston, 9–10 July 2008
Kent 175 for 6 (20 overs) (DI Stevens 69)
Warwickshire 133 for 8 (20 overs) (Yasir Arafat 3 for 29)
Kent beat Warwickshire by 42 runs

* quarter-final replay
at Chester-le-Street, 22 July 2008
Durham 163 for 8 (20 overs) (WR Smith 51, JAR Harris 3 for 41)
Glamorgan 119 (17.4 overs) (LE Plunkett 3 for 16)
Durham beat Glamorgan by 44 runs

Finals Day (Rose Bowl, 26 July 2008)
Semi-finals
Summer would no longer be the same without Twenty20 Finals Day. And in 2008 there was more at stake than ever. The two semi-final winners would gain a place in the lucrative new Champions League; the tournament winners would receive an invite to join the Stanford Super Series – worth a reputed £30,000 a player. Middlesex – the form team of the group stages (with ten wins) – had their spinners Shaun Udal and Murali Kartik to thank in the first semi-final for restricting Durham to 138 for 6. Middlesex reached the target in the 15th over. The second semi-final was all about fielding. A sloppy Essex allowed Kent to reach 173 for 7. Kent, on the other hand, excelled in the field, restricted their South East neighbours to 159 and gave themselves a shot at becoming the first side in the competition's history to defend the trophy.

Durham 138 for 6 (20 overs) (TJ Murtagh 3 for 29)
Middlesex 141 for 2 (15.4 overs) (T Henderson 59*)
Middlesex beat Durham by 8 wickets

Kent 173 for 7 (20 overs) (RS Bopara 3 for 36)
Essex 159 for 8 (20 overs) (ML Pettini 54)
Kent beat Essex by 14 runs

Top of the hops: Kent opener Joe Denly showed his immense promise, ending as the tournament's top scorer with 451 runs.

FINAL

Just as had been the case in the Indian Premier League a few months earlier, the final of the 2008 Twenty20 Cup was the best match of the tournament. Owais Shah smashed an imperious 75 off 35 deliveries and Tyron Henderson hit a more measured 43 to help Middlesex to a competitive total of 187 for 6 (the highest total in the history of the final). Kent were always in the hunt. Rob Key and Joe Denly took them past 50 within five overs, before the excellent Middlesex spin pairing of Shaun Udal and Murali Kartik stemmed the flow of runs. In the end Kent needed 28 off the final two overs; then 16 runs off the final over, to be bowled by Henderson. The South African held his nerve, Kent fell three runs short, and Middlesex collected their first domestic trophy for 15 years. But the match was far more than that: it was the perfect advert for cricket's most exciting format.

HONOURS BOARD 2008

TEAM HONOURS

FINAL
26 July 2008
At Rose Bowl, Southampton, Hampshire

Middlesex Crusaders beat Kent Spitfires by 3 runs

Middlesex Crusaders			R	B	4s	6s	SR
BA Godleman		b Yasir Arafat	1	6	0	0	16.66
*EC Joyce	c Jones	b Cook	23	12	5	0	191.66
T Henderson	c Key	b McLaren	43	33	4	2	130.30
OA Shah		b McLaren	75	35	6	5	214.28
EJG Morgan	c Tredwell	b Mahmood	23	18	2	0	127.77
DJ Malan	not out		6	8	0	0	75.00
SD Udal		b Yasir Arafat	1	3	0	0	33.33
†BJM Scott	not out		6	5	1	0	120.00
Extras	(b 5, lb 1, w 3)		9				
Total	(6 wickets, 20 overs)		187				

Fall of wickets: 1-19, 2-47, 3-83, 4-162, 5-173, 6-179
Did not bat: TJ Murtagh, M Kartik, DP Nannes
Bowling: Yasir Arafat 4-0-20-2; Azhar Mahmood 4-0-33-1; R McLaren 4-0-36-2; SJ Cook 4-0-35-1; JC Tredwell 2-0-27-0; DI Stevens 2-0-30-0

Kent Spitfires			R	B	4s	6s	SR
JL Denly	c Godleman	b Udal	31	25	5	0	124.00
*RWT Key	c Scott	b Kartik	52	30	9	1	173.33
JM Kemp	run out	(Henderson)	49	38	3	3	128.94
Yasir Arafat	run out	(Joyce)	1	1	0	0	100.00
DI Stevens	c Joyce	b Nannes	33	23	1	2	143.47
Azhar Mahmood	not out		6	4	1	0	150.00
Extras	(lb 6, w 4, nb 2)		12				
Total	(5 wickets, 20 overs)		184				

Fall of wickets: 1-89, 2-91, 3-96, 4-166, 5-184
Did not bat: M van Jaarsveld, R McLaren, †GO Jones, JC Tredwell, SJ Cook
Bowling: TJ Murtagh 4-0-32-0; DP Nannes 4-0-37-1; T Henderson 4-0-58-0; M Kartik 4-0-30-1; SD Udal 4-0-21-1

Umpires: JW Lloyds and NA Mallender
Man of the Match: *OA Shah (Middlesex)*

Highest Total

Total	Team	Overs	RR	Inns	Opposition	Ground	Date
242/3	Essex	20.0	12.10	1	Sussex	Chelmsford	24/06/2008

Biggest Margin of Victory – by runs

Margin	Winner	Target		Opposition	Ground	Date
128 runs	Essex	243		Sussex	Chelmsford	24/06/2008

By wickets

Margin	Winner	Balls Rem	Target	Overs	Opposition	Ground	Date
10 wkts	Lancashire	24	112	16.0	Derbyshire	Derby	13/06/2008

The Twenty20 Cup 2008

INDIVIDUAL HONOURS

Most Runs

Player	M	I	NO	Runs	HS	Ave	BF	SR	100	50
JL Denly (Kent)	13	13	0	451	91	34.69	379	118.99	0	5
A McGrath (Yorkshire)	9	9	2	392	72*	56.00	296	132.43	0	4
MW Goodwin (Sussex)	10	10	2	345	79*	43.12	273	126.37	0	3
RWT Key (Kent)	13	13	0	345	52	26.53	258	133.72	0	1
MA Carberry (Hampshire)	10	10	1	334	58	37.11	268	124.62	0	4
GR Napier (Essex)	12	11	1	326	152*	32.60	167	195.20	1	0
MJ Lumb (Hampshire)	10	10	0	315	63	31.50	209	150.71	0	2
ME Trescothick (Somerset)	8	8	0	306	107	38.25	185	165.40	1	1
DJ Malan (Middlesex)	12	10	5	306	103	61.20	220	139.09	1	1
P Mustard (Durham)	11	11	0	303	61	27.54	224	135.26	0	1

Highest Score

Player	Runs	Balls	4s	6s	SR	Team	Opposition	Ground	Date
GR Napier	152*	58	10	16	262.06	Essex	Sussex	Chelmsford	24/06/08
ME Trescothick	107	57	15	3	187.71	Somerset	Worcs	Taunton	22/06/08
DJ Malan	103	54	10	6	190.74	Middlesex	Lancs	The Oval	08/07/08
L Vincent	102*	63	11	3	161.90	Lancs	Derbys	Manchester	23/06/08
GM Smith	100*	62	12	2	161.29	Derbys	Yorks	Leeds	12/06/08
HH Gibbs	98	52	14	2	188.46	Glam	Northants	Northampton	22/06/08
RA White	94*	57	8	3	164.91	Northants	Gloucs	M Keynes	17/06/08
JL Denly	91	57	9	5	159.64	Kent	Essex	Beckenham	22/06/08
GA Hick	88*	58	11	1	151.72	Worcs	Gloucs	Worcester	12/06/08
MW Goodwin	79*	46	9	2	171.74	Sussex	Surrey	Hove	22/06/08

Most Wickets

Player	M	O	M	Runs	Wkts	BB	Ave	Econ	SR	4w	5w
Yasir Arafat (Kent)	13	44.0	0	341	23	4/17	14.82	7.75	11.4	2	0
T Henderson (Middlesex)	12	47.0	0	349	21	4/29	16.61	7.42	13.4	1	0
AJ Hall (Northants)	9	34.1	0	271	20	6/21	13.55	7.93	10.2	0	2
Danish Kaneria (Essex)	12	45.1	0	276	20	4/22	13.80	6.11	13.5	1	0
TJ Murtagh (Middlesex)	13	50.0	0	400	20	3/15	20.00	8.00	15.0	0	0
J Louw (Northants)	11	39.0	0	325	17	3/18	19.11	8.33	13.7	0	0
JC Tredwell (Kent)	13	41.0	1	264	16	3/9	16.50	6.43	15.3	0	0
GR Napier (Essex)	12	40.1	2	282	16	4/10	17.62	7.02	15.0	1	0
IDK Salisbury (Warks)	10	32.0	0	175	15	3/14	11.66	5.46	12.8	0	0
Abdul Razzaq (Surrey)	9	32.0	0	232	15	4/17	15.46	7.25	12.8	1	0

Best Bowling in an Innings

Player	O	M	R	W	Econ	Team	Opposition	Venue	Date
AJ Hall	3.4	0	21	6	5.72	Northants	Worcs	N'hampton	13/06/08
PD Collingwood	4.0	0	14	5	3.50	Durham	Derbyshire	Chester-le-Street	11/06/08
J Allenby	3.0	0	21	5	7.00	Leics	Lancs	Manchester	15/06/18
J Allenby	4.0	0	27	5	6.75	Leics	Derbyshire	Leicester	27/06/08
AJ Hall	4.0	0	29	5	7.25	Northants	Glamorgan	N'hampton	22/06/08
CK Langeveldt	4.0	0	9	4	2.25	Derbyshire	Yorkshire	Leeds	12/06/08
GR Napier	4.0	1	10	4	2.50	Essex	Northants	Chelmsford	07/07/08
DKH Mitchell	3.0	0	11	4	3.66	Worcs	Gloucs	Bristol	25/06/08
A Flintoff	2.0	0	12	4	6.00	Lancs	Durham	Chester-le-Street	27/06/08
G Keedy	3.4	1	15	4	4.09	Lancs	Derbyshire	Derby	16/06/08

Most Sixes

Player	No. of sixes	No. of innings
GR Napier (Essex)	28	11
T Henderson (Middlesex)	17	11
JL Denly (Kent)	16	13
DJG Sales (Northants)	14	10
Azhar Mahmood (Kent)	14	13
SM Ervine (Hampshire)	13	9
DR Smith (Sussex)	13	9
NM Carter (Warwicks)	13	10
ME Trescothick (Somerset)	12	8

Best Economy Rate (qualification 4 wickets)

Player	O	M	R	W	BB	Ave.	Econ	4	5
AG Botha (Warks)	31.0	0	163	14	3/15	11.64	5.25	0	0
SM Pollock (Durham)	38.4	1	210	13	2/15	16.15	5.43	0	0
IDK Salisbury (Warks)	32.0	0	175	15	3/14	11.66	5.46	0	0
A Flintoff (Lancs)	10.0	0	56	8	4/12	7.00	5.60	1	0
CK Langeveldt (Derbys)	21.0	1	118	8	4/9	14.75	5.61	1	0
PD Collingwood (Durham)	8.0	0	46	7	5/14	6.57	5.75	0	1
ND Doshi (Derbys)	33.4	0	198	8	3/1	24.75	5.88	0	0
G Chapple (Lancashire)	16.0	0	95	5	2/23	19.00	5.93	0	0
Danish Kaneria (Essex)	45.1	0	276	20	4/22	13.80	6.11	1	0
CW Henderson (Leics)	33.3	0	205	8	2/15	25.62	6.11	0	0

Danger man: Yasir Arafat of Kent was the leading wicket-taker in 2008 with 23 victims in 44 overs.

Twenty20 Cup Team of the Year

1. Joe Denly (Kent Spitfires)
451 runs (ave 34.69; scoring rate: 118.99)
The 22-year-old right-handed Kent opener more than lived up to his reputation as one of the brightest prospects on the county circuit by scoring four centuries in his first seven innings and ending the competition as the leading run-scorer and the only player to pass the 400-run milestone. Denly has already been selected for the England Lions team; it would appear to be only a matter of time before he receives full international recognition.

2. Marcus Trescothick (Somerset Sabres)
306 runs (ave: 38.25; scoring rate: 165.40)
Somerset may have endured an indifferent 2008 campaign, but the form of their opener, Marcus Trescothick, stood out like a beacon. A scintillating 57-ball century (107) against Worcestershire and a 32-ball 69 against Northamptonshire were the highlights, but the genial left-hander, who had announced his retirement from international cricket in March 2008, left England cricket fans with a stark reminder of the quality they would be missing at the top of the order.

3. Robert Key (Kent Spitfires, captain)
345 runs (ave: 26.53; scoring rate: 133.72)
The Kent captain ultimately failed in his bid to become the first man to lead his side to back-to-back Twenty20 Cup triumphs, but the tournament showed Robert Key to be a major player on the domestic scene. The competition's joint third-highest scorer with 345 runs — despite only recording a top score of 52 — his consistent contributions at the top of the order, coupled with his artful captaincy, did much to propel Kent towards a coveted Champions League spot.

4. Owais Shah (Middlesex Crusaders)
136 runs (ave: 45.33; scoring rate: 158.13)
Although he only played four matches for Middlesex in their march to the Twenty20 Cup, Owais Shah earns his selection in the team of the year on the strength of his scintillating performance in the final. Showing the form that has made him a regular in England's one-day teams, his brilliant 35-ball 75 (containing five sixes) helped Middlesex to a formidable 187 for 6 and went a long way to securing his county their biggest ever payday.

5. Graham Napier (Essex Eagles)
326 runs (ave: 32.60; scoring rate: 195.20); 16 wickets (ave 17.62; economy: 7.02)
By the end of the Twenty20 Cup, Graham Napier had become one of the most talked-about players on the domestic circuit. The 28-year-old enjoyed an immense competition, scoring 326 runs – including a tournament-best 152 not out against Sussex (an innings that contained a world-record 16 sixes) and taking 16 wickets to lie seventh in the wicket-taking list. His performances may well have captured the attention of both the England selectors and the Indian Premier League scouts.

6. Dawid Malan (Middlesex Crusaders)
306 runs (ave: 61.20; scoring rate: 139.09)
Dawid Malan was the find of the tournament. Prior to the 2008 season, the 20-year-old left-hander had struggled to break into the Middlesex side in all forms of the game, but given his chance in T20 he grabbed it with both hands. His impressive run in the tournament yielded 306 runs at an average of 61.20, the highlight of which came during his side's quarter-final victory over Lancashire when the youngster smashed a 54-ball 103. A great future awaits.

7. Tyron Henderson* (Middlesex Crusaders)
281 runs (ave: 40.14; scoring rate: 180.12); 21 wickets (average 16.61; economy: 7.42)
A swashbuckling performer with the bat and an effective contributor with the ball, Tyron Henderson put in some eye-catching performances for Middlesex. He scored an unbeaten 59 off 21 balls (including seven sixes) in Middlesex's semi-final win over Durham, ended as the competition's second-highest wicket-taker (with 21), and held his nerve when asked to bowl the last over in the final against Kent to hand Middlesex their first piece of silverware for 15 years.

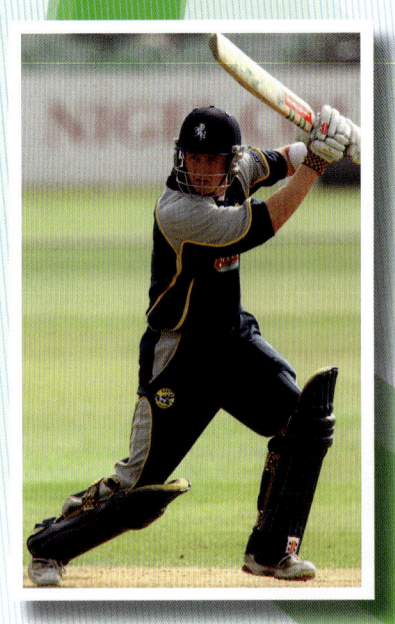

Driving force: Consistent run-scoring and astute captaincy from Robert Key were pivotal to Kent's march to the final.

Pretty in Pink: The 2008 Twenty20 Cup marked a remarkable turnaround for veteran off-spinner Shaun Udal, who was coaxed out of retirement by Middlesex.

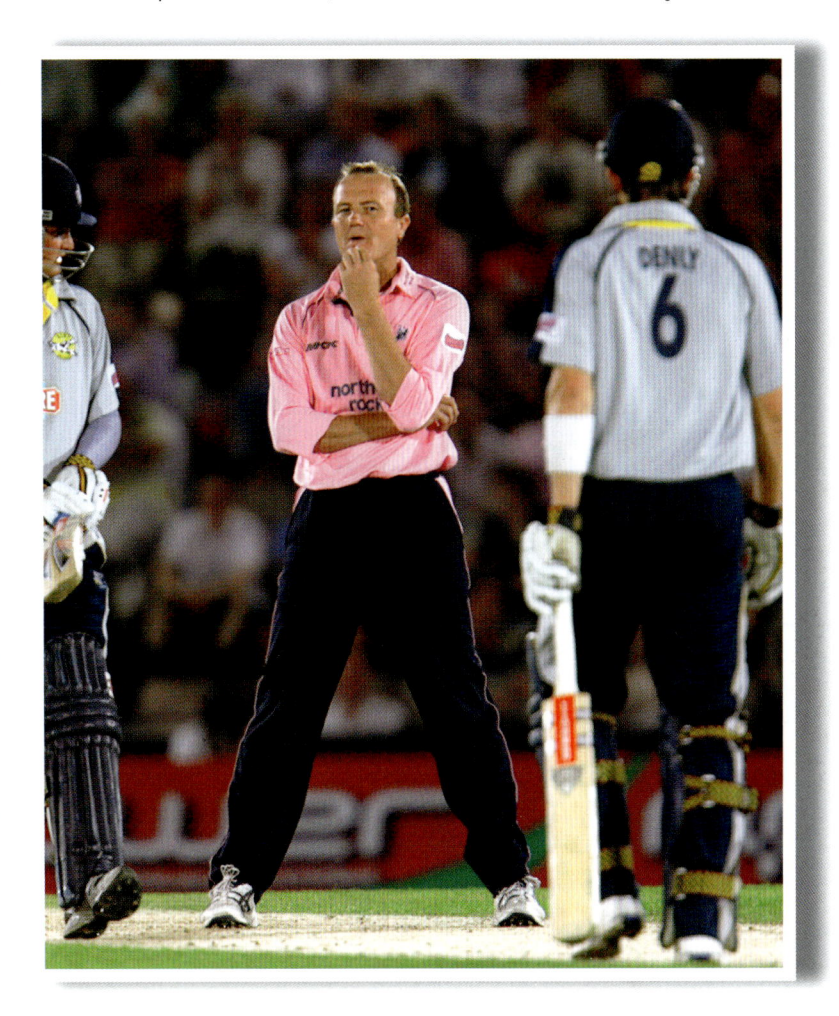

8. Phil Mustard (Durham Dynamos, wicketkeeper)
303 runs (ave: 27.54; scoring rate: 135.26)
Following a successful 2007 season with Durham – which earned him international recognition during England's 2007–08 tours – wicketkeeper Phil Mustard enjoyed his best Twenty20 Cup to date. Consistent contributions at the top of the Durham order saw him amass 303 runs, with a top score of 61. Long touted as the answer to England's long-standing wicketkeeper problems, he went a long way to putting his name at the top of a long list of contenders.

9. Andrew Flintoff (Lancashire Lightning)
75 runs (ave: 18.75; scoring rate: 129.31); 8 wickets (ave: 7.00; economy rate: 5.60)
England's talisman used the Twenty20 Cup as his comeback trail from an injury nightmare – one that has kept him out of an England Test shirt since January 2007 – and reminded everyone of what a special player he is. He shone for Lancashire during their losing quarter-final against Middlesex, taking 3 for 16 and smashing 53. The performance confirmed that, when fit, Flintoff would be a shoo-in in any team in the world, in any format of the game.

10. Yasir Arafat* (Kent Spitfires)
130 runs (ave: 21.66; scoring rate: 154.76); 23 wickets (ave: 14.82; economy: 7.75)
The 26-year-old medium-pacer, who was awarded a central contract by Pakistan for the first time in 2007, did much to confirm his status as a player for the future by taking a tournament-leading 23 wickets during Kent's march to the final. Also capable of making useful contributions with the bat – he batted at No.4 in the final against Middlesex – he could be a highly sought-after player when the next round of Indian Premier League matches comes around.

11. Shaun Udal (Middlesex Crusaders)
99 runs (ave: 33.00; scoring rate: 139.43); 12 wickets (ave: 24.91; economy: 6.22)
He will have reached 40 years of age by the start of the 2009 Twenty20 Cup, but for Shaun Udal the 2008 Twenty20 Cup was a competition to remember. Used with the ball as the mid-innings "strangler", the veteran off-spinner excelled and did much to lead Middlesex to the Cup and a place in the lucrative Champions League: his four overs in the semi-final cost a miserly 18 runs; in the final he conceded a mere 21.

* one of two permitted overseas players.

Women's Twenty20

Recent years have been tough for women's cricket. Interest in the game remains low, there is little money available and, to a great extent, circumstances mean that an international match is little more than a parade of skilled and highly dedicated amateurs. The rise of T20 could not have come at a better time for women's cricket.

The spread of central player contracts may have done much to revolutionize women's cricket – the English and Australian boards now pay their players and the Indian board seems certain to follow suit – but such changes cannot come quickly enough. South Africa's star player Johmari Logtenberg quit the game in 2008 at 18 years of age to take up golf, claiming that she could not play for charity. Other players could be set to follow.

And yet women's cricket has often stolen a march on its male counterpart. The first Women's World Cup was staged in England, two years before the men's inaugural tournament, and the first international T20 match also occurred in the women's game: England took on New Zealand at Hove on 5 August 2004, some six months before men's T20 internationals got off the ground.

Twenty20 cricket could well be the ideal vehicle in which to explore better ways of marketing the women's game. The experiments have already started: women's matches have been used as curtain-raisers to a men's match; internationals have been staged at outgrounds – such as when England took on New Zealand in August 2007 at a packed ground in Bath; and the 2009 ICC Women's World Twenty20 will be staged alongside the men's tournament. The competition should provide the women's game with tremendous exposure. It is down to the game's administrators to make the most of it.

In the meantime, the women's international T20 fixture list has still to gather pace. Test matches and one-day internationals still dominate the calendar and fewer than 20 T20 internationals have been staged since that match in Hove. During that time Australia, world champions in the 50-over game, have shown their liking for the 20-over format, losing only once – to New Zealand. The Kiwis, along with England and India, continue to breathe hard over Australia's shoulder. As is the case in the men's game, the fixture list will become more hectic in the build-up to the ICC Women's World Twenty20: but there is little doubt that 2009 remains an incredibly important year for the women's game.

Record-setter: New Zealand star Amy Satterthwaite's 6 for 17 against England at Taunton remains the best bowling in Women's T20 international cricket.

Women's T20 international results (up to 1 September 2008)

Winner	Result	Margin	Match	Venue	Date
New Zealand	won	9 runs	England v New Zealand	Hove	05/08/2004
Australia	won	7 wickets	England v Australia	Taunton	02/09/2005
India	won	8 wickets	England v India	Derby	05/08/2006
	tied		Australia v New Zealand	Brisbane	18/10/2006
Australia	won	1 run	Australia v New Zealand	Darwin	19/07/2007
New Zealand	won	97 runs	New Zealand v South Africa	Taunton	10/08/2007
England	won	86 runs	England v South Africa	Taunton	10/08/2007
England	won	20 runs	England v New Zealand	Bath	12/08/2007
England	won	5 wickets	England v New Zealand	Bath	13/08/2008
New Zealand	won	36 runs	England v New Zealand	Taunton	16/08/2008
Australia	won	21 runs	Australia v England	Melbourne	01/02/2008
New Zealand	won	4 wickets	New Zealand v Australia	Lincoln	06/03/2008
West Indies	won	75 runs	Ireland v West Indies	Dublin	27/06/2008
West Indies	won	7 wickets	Netherlands v West Indies	Utrecht	01/07/2008
West Indies	won	58 runs	Netherlands v West Indies	Deventer	06/07/2008
South Africa	won	8 runs	Ireland v South Africa	Crowthorne	01/08/2008

Leading Run-scorers

Player	M	I	NO	R	HS	Ave	BF	SR	100	50
CM Edwards (England)	7	6	0	212	64	35.33	176	120.45	0	2
SC Taylor (England)	8	8	1	212	43	30.28	174	121.83	0	0
KL Rolton (Australia)	5	5	2	193	96*	64.33	149	129.53	0	2
SACA King (West Indies)	3	3	1	171	79*	85.50	118	144.91	0	2
AL Mason (NZ)	7	7	1	168	54*	28.00	119	141.17	0	1

Highest Score

Player	Runs	Balls	4s	6s	SR	Team	Opposition	Venue	Date
KL Rolton	96*	53	16	1	181.13	Australia	England	Taunton	02/09/2005
SR Taylor	90	49	12	2	183.67	WI	Ireland	Dublin	27/06/2008
SACA King	79*	57	7	1	138.59	WI	Netherlands	Deventer	06/07/2008
KL Rolton	71*	59	11	0	120.33	Australia	NZ	Brisbane	18/10/2006
R Dhar	66*	69	6	0	95.65	India	England	Derby	05/08/2006

Leading Wicket-takers

Player	M	O	M	R	W	BB	Ave	Econ	SR	4	5
JL Gunn (England)	8	26.0	0	182	9	4/9	20.22	7.00	17.3	1	0
NJ Browne (NZ)	8	22.0	0	129	8	3/14	16.12	5.86	16.5	0	0
SK Burke (NZ)	7	23.0	1	149	7	3/15	21.28	6.47	19.7	0	0
HM Watson (NZ)	8	28.0	2	152	7	3/13	21.71	5.42	24.0	0	0
AE Satterthwaite (NZ)	4	4.0	0	17	6	6/17	2.83	4.25	4.0	0	1

Best Bowling in an Innings

Player	O	M	R	W	Econ	Team	Opposition	Ground	Date
AE Satterthwaite	4.0	0	17	6	4.25	NZ	England	Taunton	16/08/2007
JL Gunn	2.0	0	9	4	4.50	England	NZ	Taunton	10/08/2007
EA Perry	4.0	0	20	4	5.00	Australia	England	Melbourne	01/02/2008
A Mohammed	4.0	0	20	4	5.00	WI	Netherlands	Utrecht	01/07/2008
RA Birch	4.0	0	27	4	6.75	England	NZ	Hove	05/08/2004

Heavy hitter: England captain Charlotte Edwards is the leading run-scorer in women's T20 internationals.

Global Round-Up of Domestic Twenty20 Cricket

Twenty20 cricket has provided the domestic game around the world with the financial shot in the arm it so desperately needed. Six years after the launch of the Twenty20 Cup in England, every Test-playing nation, bar Bangladesh, hosts its own 20-over tournament – and each has become a highlight of the domestic calendar.

In South Africa, the Standard Bank Pro 20 series may have been book-ended to the end of the season – meaning that it took place in colder conditions, had to compete with the attractions of the Super 14 rugby competition, the start of the Indian Premier League, and the absence of many international stars until the knockout rounds – but it still managed to capture the public's imagination like no other domestic tournament. In the end, the Titans made the most of their returning stars – AB de Villiers, the Morkel brothers and Dale Steyn – and went on to beat the Dolphins in the final by 18 runs to collect the trophy for a second time.

Victoria continued to reign supreme in Australia, collecting their third straight Twenty20 title with a comfortable 32-run win over Western Australia in the final. Dirk Nannes was the star of the show, producing a fast and accurate spell of bowling to take 4 for 23.

Despite being the biggest crowd-puller in recent years (the finals have pulled in crowds of over 30,000), Pakistan's domestic 20-over competition – the ABN-AMRO Twenty20 – was postponed to later in the year after administrators failed to find a place for it in its domestic calendar. With the threat of a mass exodus of players to India's two 20-over competitions (the Indian Cricket League and the Indian Premier League), it is a situation that needs addressing, and quickly, for the Pakistan Cricket Board.

There were no such problems in New Zealand, where Central Districts, led by Geoff Barnett (36) and Jacob Oram (34 off 23 balls) cruised past Northern Districts' disappointing total of 148 for 8 with a comfortable 21 balls to spare to pick up the State Twenty20 trophy for the first time – they had been forced to share it with Wellington in the 2006–07 season after rain had forced the abandonment of the final without a ball being bowled.

Over in the Caribbean, Trinidad and Tobago brushed aside memories of a painful five-wicket defeat to Guyana in the final of the 2006 Stanford 20/20 to crush Jamaica by nine wickets and collect the trophy – and the US$1 million prize money – for the first time. In a one-sided final, Dave Mohammed took 4 for 20 as Jamaica slumped to a paltry 91 all out; Trinidad and Tobago required just 9.2 overs to reach the target, with opener William Perkins slamming an unbeaten half-century.

In Sri Lanka, Jeevantha Kalutanga was the star of the show, smashing 78 off 45 balls and taking 2 for 33 as Wayamba beat Ruhuna by 31 runs to win the inaugural Inter-State Twenty20 final – the tournament replaced an inter-club competition that had begun in 2005–06.

In Zimbabwe, Easterns beat Westerns by seven runs to claim the inaugural Provincial A Twenty20 tournament.

Australia (KFC Twenty20)

Year	Winners	Runners-up	Result
2005–06	Victoria	New South Wales	Victoria beat New South Wales by 93 runs
2006–07	Victoria	Tasmania	Victoria beat Tasmania by 10 runs
2007–08	Victoria	Western Australia	Victoria beat Western Australia by 32 runs

India (Inter-State Twenty20)

Year	Winners	Runners-up	Result
2006–07	Tamil Nadu	Punjab	Tamil Nadu beat Punjab by 2 wickets

The competition was superseded in 2007–08 by the advent of the Indian Premier League

New Zealand (State Twenty20)

Year	Winners	Runners-up	Result
2005–06	Canterbury	Auckland	Canterbury beat Auckland by 6 wickets
2006–07			*Central Districts v Wellington abandoned (trophy shared)*
2007–08	Central Districts	Northern Districts	Central Districts beat Northern Districts by 5 wickets

Pakistan (ABN-AMRO Twenty20)

Year	Winners	Runners-up	Result
2004–05	Faisalabad Wolves	Karachi Dolphins	Faisalabad beat Karachi by 2 wickets
2005–06	Sialkot Stallions	Faisalabad Wolves	Sialkot beat Faisalabad by 6 wickets
2006–07	Sialkot Stallions	Karachi Dolphins	Sialkot beat Karachi by 14 runs
2007–08	Sialkot Stallions	Karachi Dolphins	Sialkot beat Karachi by 7 wickets *(Played in October 2008)*

Sri Lanka (Inter-Provincial Twenty20)

Year	Winners	Runners-up	Result
2005–06	Sinhalese SC	Chilaw Marians CC	Sinhalese SC beat Chilaw Marians CC by 7 runs (D/L)
2006–07	Ragama CC	Saracens SC	Ragama CC beat Saracens SC by 111 runs
2007–08	Wayamba	Ruhuna	Wayamba beat Ruhuna by 31 runs

South Africa (Standard Bank Pro 20 Series)

Year	Winners	Runners-up	Result
2003–04	Eagles	Eastern Cape	Eagles beat Eastern Cape by 7 runs (D/L Method)
2004–05	Titans	Warriors	Titans beat Warriors by 8 wickets
2005–06	Eagles	Cape Cobras	Eagles beat Cape Cobras by 6 wickets
2006–07	Lions	Cape Cobras	Lions beat Cape Cobras by 6 wickets
2007–08	Titans	Dolphins	Titans beat Dolphins by 18 runs

West Indies (Stanford 20/20)

Year	Winners	Runners-up	Result
2006	Guyana	Trinidad and Tobago	Guyana beat Trinidad and Tobago by 5 wickets
2008	Trinidad and Tobago	Jamaica	Trinidad and Tobago beat Jamaica by 9 wickets

Zimbabwe (Provincial A Twenty20)

Year	Winners	Runners-up	Result
2007–08	Easterns	Westerns	Easterns beat Westerns by 7 runs

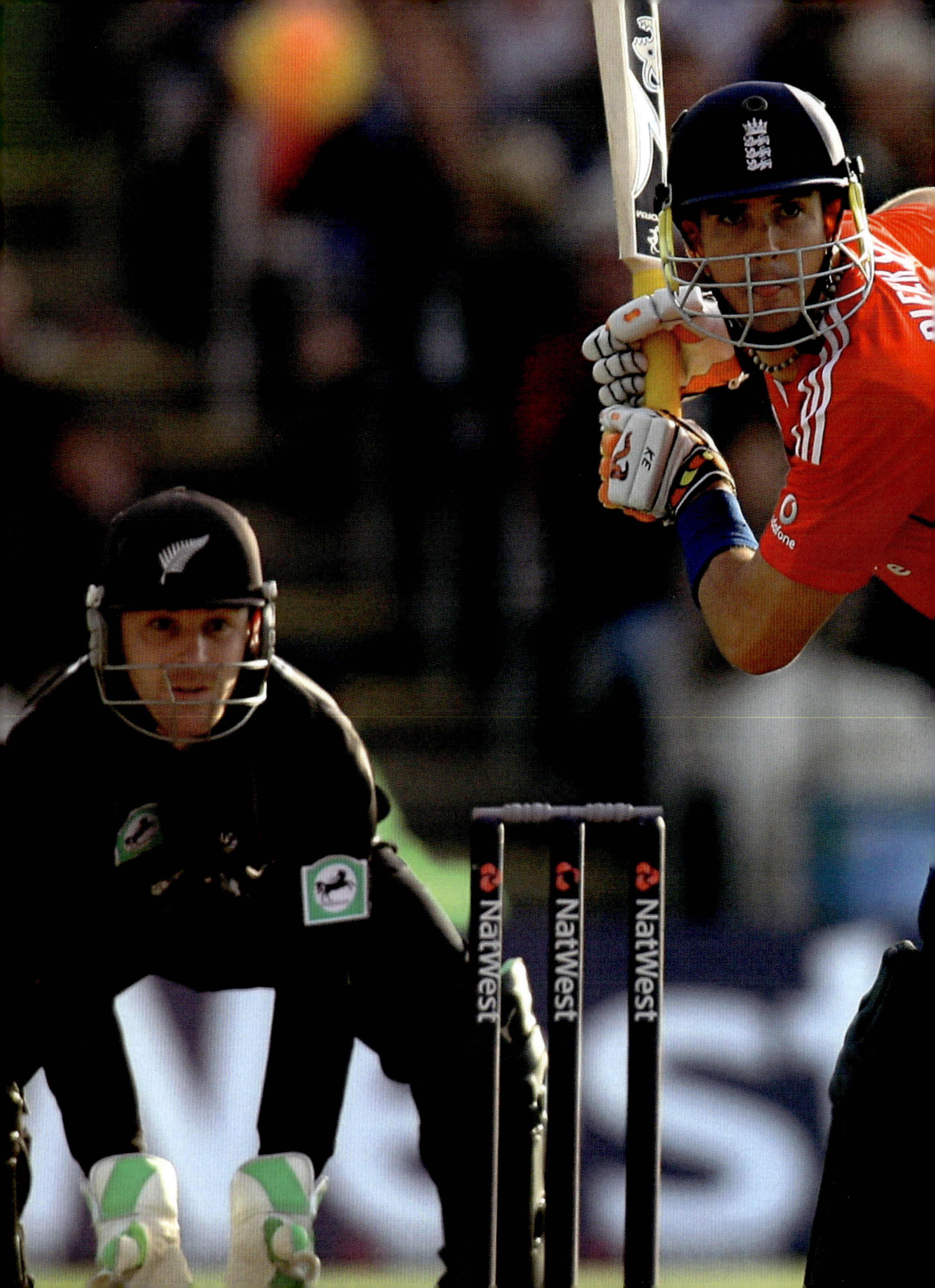
NatWest
NatWest
NatWest

Preview of the Season 2009

This is a big year for Twenty20 cricket. All eyes will be focused on the second edition of the Indian Premier League; another county side will have a shot at a place in the Champions League; players in county cricket will be desperate to impress national selectors and earn a place in the second edition of Allen Stanford's million-dollar-a-man shootout; and England will host the second ICC World Twenty20. Can Rajasthan hang on to the crown they won in 2008? Will Middlesex become the first back-to-back winners of the Twenty20 Cup? And can India produce another fairy-tale performance to defend their world crown? It promises to be fun-packed action all the way.

England expects: Powered by the big hitting of Kevin Pietersen, England will be hoping to win the ICC World Twenty20 championship when it is played on home soil in June 2009.

ICC WorldTwenty20 2009

Twenty-six matches in 16 days played at three of the game's most traditional venues. Twelve teams will travel to England in June 2009 for the second staging of the ICC World Twenty20 championship. The expectation will be huge. Can India defend the trophy they won so dramatically in 2007? Will Australia collect the only international prize missing from their impressive haul? Can England make the most of home advantage to secure their first-ever world crown? Or will it be the turn of South Africa or New Zealand to bask in the spotlight for the first time? The answers will have to wait, but rest assured it will be crash-bang-wallop excitement all the way.

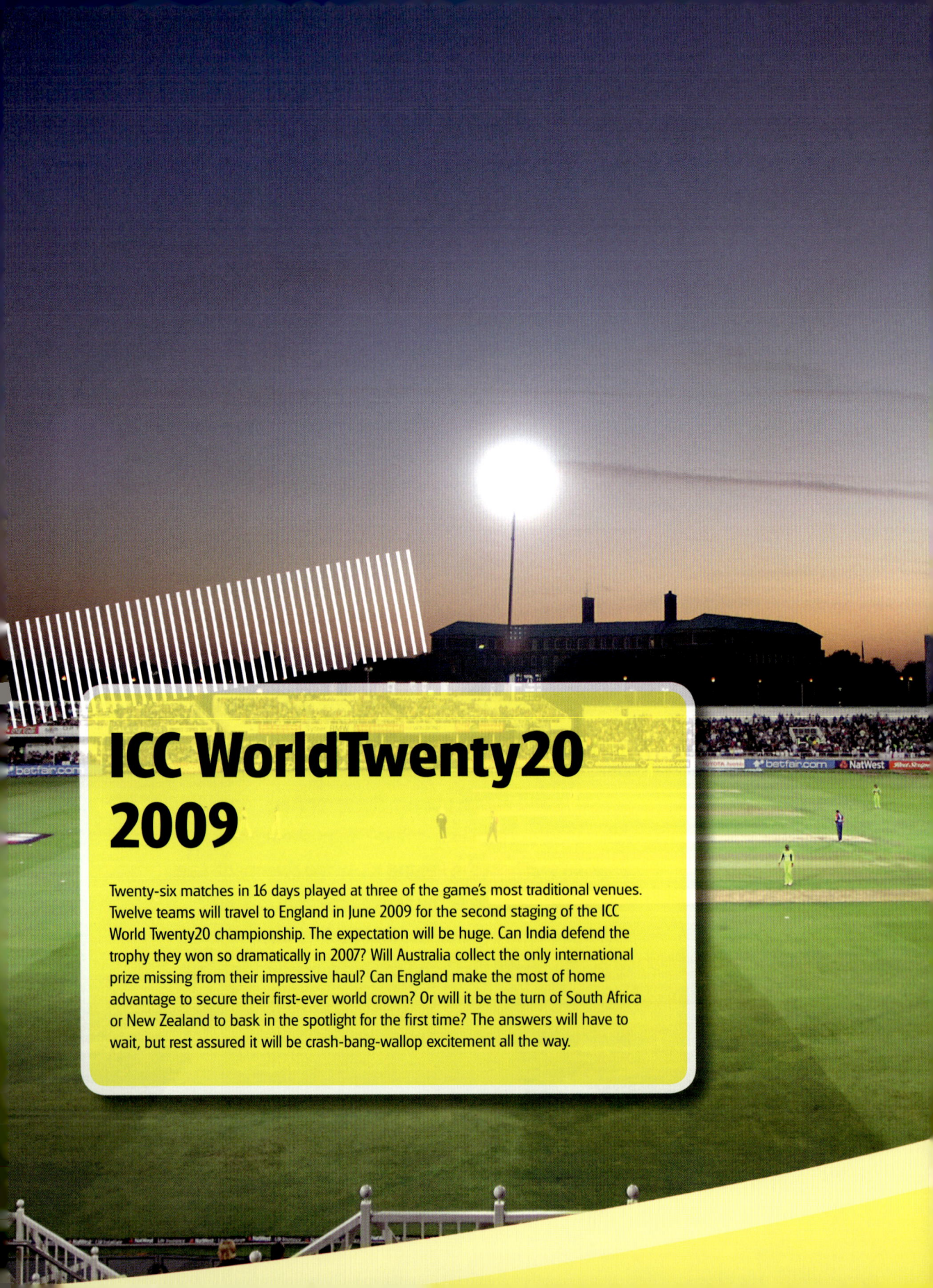

Masters of mayhem:
Top: **Jacob Oram**: One of New Zealand's most feared batters, he can send the ball enormous distances.
Above: **Andrew Flintoff:** England will be hoping that Freddie can stay fit and healthy for the whole summer and make a big impact in the short and long forms of the game.

The Venues

The 20-over game may be the new format on the international cricket block, but the ICC World Twenty20 will be contested at three of cricket's most venerable venues. Lord's, The Oval and Trent Bridge are grounds that already resound with the history of the game; the events of June 2009 are sure to provide another entertaining chapter.

Lord's
St John's Wood, London

Capacity: 30,000
End names: Pavilion, Nursery
Home teams: MCC, Middlesex
Matches: Netherlands v England (Group B, 5/6/09); New Zealand v South Africa (Group D, 9/6/09); B1 v C2 (Super Eights, 12/6/09); A1 v C1 (Super Eights, 12/6/09); Final (21/6/09)
Getting there: Underground: St John's Wood, Warwick Avenue and Baker Street stations are near; Rail: Marylebone is about one mile away; Car: inadvisable and expensive – parking spaces are at a premium; Buses: more than a dozen pass by or close to the ground.

Opened in 1814 by Thomas Lord, after whom it is named, Lord's remains the spiritual home of cricket and the highlight of any player's career. It offers a blend of old and new – the Pavilion (built in 1890) stands at one end of the ground; the state-of-the-art media centre (known as the "gherkin" when it opened in 1990) looms at the other; Father Time casts his eye over proceedings from one side of the ground; on the other is the uniquely designed Mound Stand, which opened in 1987. Lord's is a ground of firsts: the first first-class fixture was played here in 1827 (Oxford v Cambridge); the first televised Test match was staged here (England v Australia in 1938); and the ground hosted the first-ever 50-over World Cup final in 1975 (Australia v West Indies). Lord's has seen it all and it is a worthy venue for the 2009 World Twenty20 final.

Lord's: The home of cricket will play host to the second ICC World Twenty20 final.

The Oval
Kennington, London

Capacity: 23,500
End names: Pavilion, Vauxhall
Home team: Surrey CCC
Matches: Scotland v New Zealand (Group D, 6/6/09); Australia v West Indies (Group C, 6/6/09); Scotland v South Africa (Group D, 7/6/09); England v Pakistan (Group B, 7/6/09); C1 v D2 (Super Eights, 13/6/09); D1 v B1 (Super Eights, 13/6/09); B2 v C1 (Super Eights, 15/6/09); B1 v A2 (Super Eights, 15/6/09); Semi-final (19/6/09)
Getting there: Tube: Oval underground station is 200 yards away from the ground; Train: Vauxhall station is less than a mile away from the ground; Car: inadvisable and expensive – parking spaces are at a premium.

The Oval, situated in Kennington, south London, is another stately English ground that oozes history. It played host to football's first-ever FA Cup final in 1872 and was the scene of the first-ever Test match played on English soil (England v Australia in September 1880 – a match that saw WG Grace slam a century on debut). It was the ground where the legend of the Ashes was born; and the one that saw the great Donald Bradman bow out of Test cricket on an uncharacteristically disappointing note. Dominated by the 1890-built pavilion at one end of the ground, and the towering gasometers that dwarf the ground on the east side, The Oval has undergone major, and much-needed, redevelopment work in recent years. Traditionally one of the faster-paced wickets in England – expect to see plenty of runs when the 2009 World Twenty20 comes to town.

Trent Bridge
Nottingham

Capacity: 17,000
End names: Pavilion, Radcliffe Road
Home team: Nottinghamshire CCC
Matches: Bangladesh v India (Group A, 6/6/09); Bangladesh v Ireland (Group A, 8/6/09); Australia v Sri Lanka (Group C, 8/6/09); India v Ireland (Group A, 10/6/09); Sri Lanka v West Indies (Group C, 10/6/09); A2 v D1 (Super Eights, 11/6/09); B2 v D2 (Super Eights, 11/6/09); D1 v C2 (Super Eights, 16/6/09); D2 v A1 (Super Eights, 16/6/09); Semi-final (18/6/09)
Getting there: Train: mainline station at Nottingham; Car: limited parking spaces are available near the ground.

First opened in 1841, Trent Bridge had to wait more than 50 years before its first opportunity to stage a Test match (England v Australia in 1899), but it has since gone on to become one of the most popular venues in the country. It is also a venue that helped nurture the careers of some of the greatest names in the game: Garfield Sobers, Clive Rice and Richard Hadlee all spent years plying their trade – and honing their skills – with Nottinghamshire in English county cricket. The ground has undergone major redevelopment in recent years, with the new Radcliffe Road and Fox Road stands – built at a cost of approaching £10 million – providing some of the best cricket-viewing facilities in England. The ground may no longer be a regular on the Test circuit, but Trent Bridge is a familiar destination for T20 cricket: it has hosted the Twenty20 Cup finals day on two occasions.

Trent Bridge: Much revamped in recent years, Nottinghamshire's home provides some of the best viewing facilities in England.

The Main Contenders: India (Group A)

Few thought India capable of even making it as far as the semi-finals of the ICC World Twenty20 in 2007. They had only ever played one Twenty20 international, had suffered an early World Cup exit in the Caribbean just six months earlier and travelled to South Africa with an inexperienced squad. Instead, they played out of their skins and ended the tournament as the inaugural T20 world champions.

Yuvraj Singh: The first person to hit six sixes in an over in a Twenty20 match.

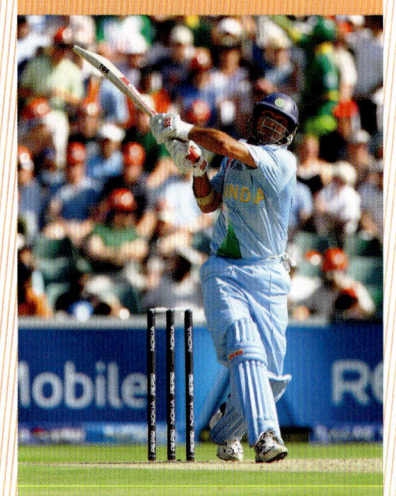

Coach: Gary Kirsten
Captain: Mahendra Singh Dhoni
Matches: P10, W6, L2, Tied 1, NR 1
Win percentage: 0.600
Highest total: 218 for 4, v England at Durban, 19 September 2007
Lowest total: 74 all out, v Australia at Melbourne, 1 February 2008
Most runs: Gautam Gambhir (299)
Highest score: 75 – Gautam Gambhir, v Pakistan at Johannesburg, 24 September 2007
Most wickets: RP Singh (13)
Best bowling: 4 for 13 – RP Singh, v South Africa at Durban, 20 September 2007
Best economy rate (qualification: four wickets): RP Singh (6.82)
2007 T20 World Cup performance: Champions

In hindsight, Sachin Tendulkar, Rahul Dravid and Sourav Ganguly's decision to opt out of the ICC World Twenty20 provided a number of India's lesser lights with an opportunity to step out of the shadows cast by those cricketing giants and make a name for themselves. The problem was, their tournament was in danger of being over before a ball had even been bowled.

A no-result against Scotland left India's players with a simple equation. A win over arch-rivals Pakistan would see them through to the second phase; a defeat could send them tumbling out of the competition. In what turned out to be a fantastic advert for the fledgling game, the two evenly matched sides served up a classic, tying the game, before India won an unnecessary bowl-out 3–0 to ensure progress to the second phase.

The match against Pakistan may have been entertaining, but it did little to dispel any doubts about India's true pedigree in the 20-over format of the game, and a 10-run defeat to New Zealand in their next match only increased the number of doubters. But, as in all fairy-tales, heroes stand up to be counted when it matters, and India's march to the world crown could well have picked up pace the moment Andrew Flintoff decided to have a few words with Yuvraj Singh during India's crunch encounter with England.

It was the end of the 17th over. India were heading for a respectable, if not intimidating, score. But then Flintoff and Yuvraj Singh exchanged opinions. What was said remains unknown, but a clearly irked Yuvraj then laid into Stuart Broad, becoming only the fourth man in history to hit six sixes in an over and propelling India to a match-winning total of 218 for 4. England made a good fist of the chase, reaching 200 for 6, but India carried the momentum gained from Yuvraj's knock through the rest of the tournament.

Rohit Sharma (50) and RP Singh (4 for 13) shone as India beat South Africa by 37 runs to end the hosts' interest in the tournament. Yuvraj (70) then stole the headlines as India beat Australia by 15 runs to progress to the final. And then came that dream victory over Pakistan, with Gautam Gambhir starring on this occasion with a superlative 75.

India's win sparked an unprecedented change in cricket. A new generation of Indian players became heroes to one billion of their estatic countrymen. The Indian Cricket Board handed the victorious squad a win bonus amounting to US$3 million and, within six months, had set up a Twenty20 league in which their new-found stars could display their talents (and earn previously unheard-of sums of money).

By the time of the ICC World Twenty20 2009, the Indian players, with two seasons of the Indian Premier League under their belts, will be among the most experienced T20 players in the game. They will start the defence of their crown among the pre-tournament favourites. Unfortunately, that is a tag with which India have never been comfortable.

Defending an unlikely crown

MS Dhoni: The wicketkeeper-batsman's lead-from-the front style has galvanized the Indian team.

STAR PLAYER:
Mahendra Singh Dhoni
Born: 7 July 1981, Ranchi, Bihar, India
Matches: 10 **Innings:** 9 **Runs:** 172 **Ave:** 24.57
Scoring rate: 111.68
Highest score: 45 (v South Africa at Cape Town, 20 September 2007)

Mahendra Singh Dhoni proved an inspirational choice to lead an inexperienced India squad at the ICC World Twenty20 in 2007. He made crucial decisions at the right time as India collected their first world crown since 1983. A swashbuckling performer with the bat (his unbeaten 183 against Sri Lanka in Jaipur in October 2005 is the highest score by a wicketkeeper in one-day international history) and a solid gloveman behind the stumps, he has become the new golden boy of Indian cricket, as evidenced by the staggering US$1.5 million IPL franchise Chennai Super Kings paid to secure his services in February 2008.

SUPPORTING CAST
Gautam Gambhir: He used India's success in South Africa as a platform to cement a place in the national set-up and has become India's most consistent batsman in all forms of one-day cricket.
Irfan Pathan: The man dubbed the best Indian fast bowler since Kapil Dev proved his worth with a man-of-the-match-winning 3 for 16 in the 2007 final against Pakistan.
Virender Sehwag: An explosive operator at the top of the Indian order. Yet to find his feet in T20 international cricket, but more than capable of destroying any bowling attack.
RP Singh: India's most prolific and economical performer in the 20-over format of the game. He is a mainstay of the Indian attack.
Yuvraj Singh: Only the fourth man in history to hit six sixes in an over – and the first in Twenty20 cricket – Yuvraj can produce match-winning fireworks from India's middle order.

The Main Contenders: Bangladesh (Group A)

Success in the Test arena has proved elusive for Bangladesh – they have won just once since their elevation to Test status in 2000 – but with over 40 one-day international wins to their name, the Tigers have proved more competitive in the shorter format of the game. They travelled to the ICC World Twenty20 2007 with high hopes ... and with good reason.

Mashrafe Mortaza: A seven-year veteran of the Bangladeshi team, the swashbuckling batsman is still only 25.

Coach: Jamie Siddons
Captain: Mohammad Ashraful
Matches: P9, W3, L6, Tied 0, NR 0
Win percentage: 0.333
Highest total: 166 all out, v Kenya at Khulna Division Stadium, 28 November 2006
Lowest total: 83 all out, v Sri Lanka at Johannesburg, 18 September 2007
Most runs: Aftab Ahmed (215)
Highest score: 81 – Nazimuddin, v Pakistan at Nairobi, 2 September 2007
Most wickets: Abdur Razzak (14)
Best bowling: 4 for 34 – Shakib Al Hasan, v West Indies at Johannesburg, 13 September 2007
Best economy rate (qualification: four wickets): Abdur Razzak (6.40)
2007 T20 World Cup performance: Second phase

The 2007 World Cup in the Caribbean had been a breakthrough moment for Bangladesh cricket. A heavy loss to Sri Lanka was punctuated by an historic five-wicket win over India and a more comfortable seven-wicket victory over Bermuda to secure progress to the second phase of an international tournament for the first time. The wins may have ended there – Bangladesh were outclassed in the Super Eights, losing all their games (including an embarrassing 74-run defeat to Ireland) – but the tournament showed progress had been made. The challenge was to turn the occasional shock win into a consistent string of victories against cricket's big boys.

And they started the tournament in magnificent fashion. Disciplined bowling in their opening group game restricted the West Indies to 164 for 8 and Bangladesh set about the run-chase in style. Mohammad Ashraful hit the fastest 50 in international T20 cricket (off 20 balls) en route to 61, Aftab Ahmed (62 not out) supported his captain ably and the Tigers eased past the target with an eye-catching two overs to spare. Bangladesh had secured progress to the second phase of a major international competition for the second consecutive tournament. Could they improve on their performances in the Caribbean?

The answer was a resounding no. It may only have been a dead-rubber match, but South Africa proved an insurmountable step up in class for Bangladesh. The Tigers started in express fashion, hammering their first 38 runs in boundaries, but then the wickets started to fall, Bangladesh limped to 144 all out and South Africa eased past the total with seven wickets and seven balls to spare.

The clinical fashion of South Africa's victory seemed to take the wind out of Bangladesh's sails. They performed well on a sluggish pitch in Johannesburg to restrict Sri Lanka to 147 for 5, but then succumbed meekly to 83 all out in 15.5 overs. Against Pakistan they failed to capitalize on debutant Junaid Siddique's 49-ball 71, posted 140 all out, and lost by four wickets. The Tigers' tournament was over.

If Bangladesh had hoped to use the first-ever T20 international to be played in Pakistan, in April 2008, as a springboard to greater things following their creditable showing in South Africa, then they were in for a rude awakening. Pakistan amassed a mighty 203 for 5; Bangladesh subsided in the 16th over to 101 all out.

It is not all bad news for the Tigers. They have a young side containing serious talent. Captain Mohammad Ashraful can lead from the front against any attack in the world; Aftab Ahmed and Nazimuddin show immense promise with the bat; and Morshrafe Mortaza and Shakib Al Hasan with the ball. Progress to the second phase in consecutive global tournaments has signalled Bangladesh's emergence among the world's elite nations. However, the ultimate challenge, to find the formula to take them to the top of the world cricket tree, continues to elude them.

Minnows still waiting to find their bite

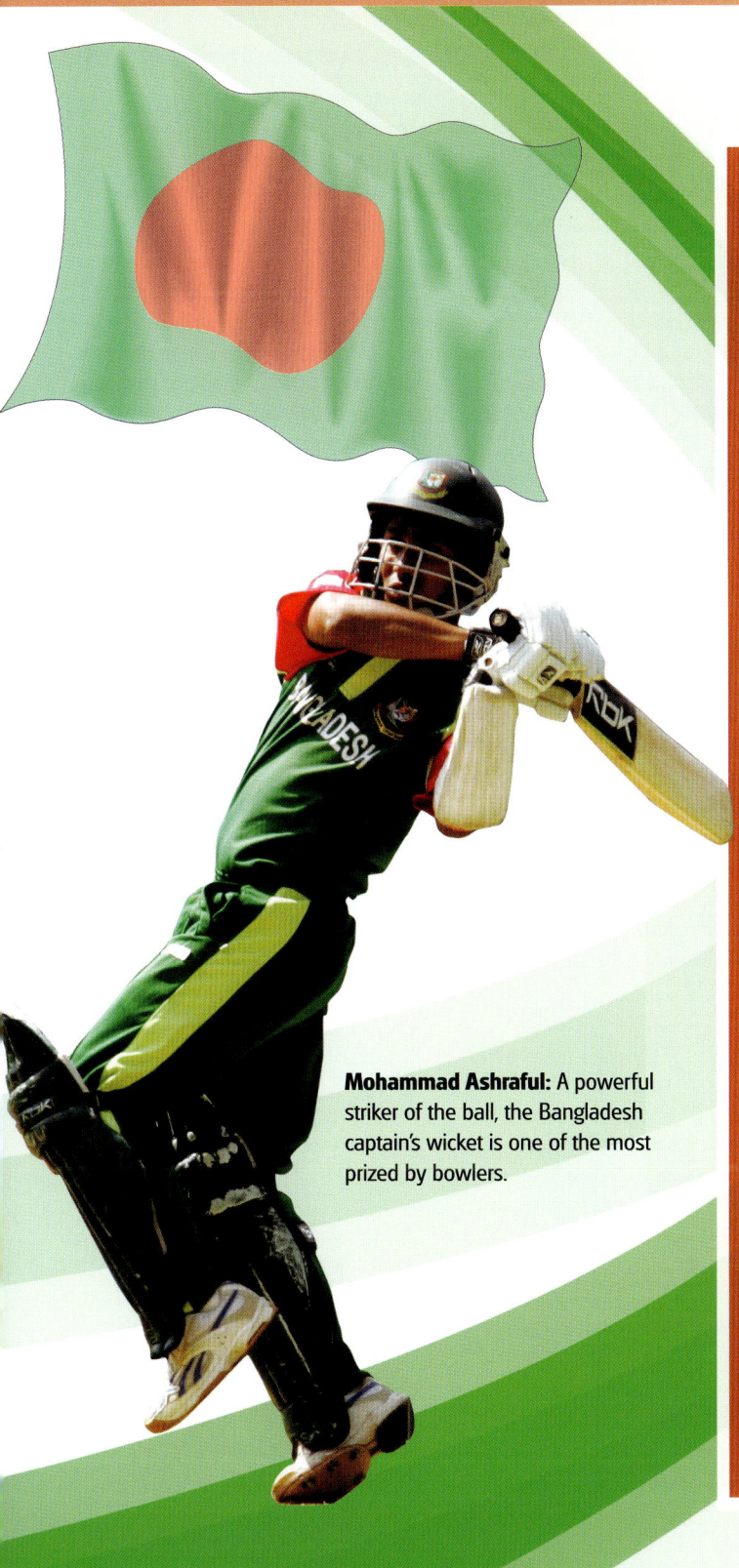

Mohammad Ashraful: A powerful striker of the ball, the Bangladesh captain's wicket is one of the most prized by bowlers.

STAR PLAYER:
Mohammad Ashraful
Born: 7 July 1984, Dhaka, Bangladesh
Matches: 8 **Innings:** 8 **Runs:** 143 **Ave:** 17.87
Scoring rate: 172.28
Highest score: 61 (v West Indies at Johannesburg, 13 September 2007)

Mohammad Ashraful burst on to the international cricket scene in September 2001 when, aged 17 years 61 days, he became the youngest player in Test history to score a century. He overcame initial struggles to cement a permanent place in the Bangladesh line-up and has gone on to become the leading light of Bangladesh cricket. A swashbuckling batsman with a full array of shots, he became the national captain in 2006 at the tender age of 22 and continues to lead from the front, as seen by his 20-ball half-century against the West Indies at the 2007 World Twenty20 that secured his side a shock win.

SUPPORTING CAST
Abdur Razzak: The latest from the long Bangladesh production line of left-arm spinners. With his high action and deadly accuracy, he performs a crucial role with the ball.
Aftab Ahmed: His refreshing all-out attacking approach at the top of the order can get Bangladesh off to a flying start. He needs to add consistency to his game.
Mashrafe Mortaza: A talismanic all-rounder for Bangladesh in recent years who has played a major role in more than one upset.
Nazimuddin: He may have endured a difficult World Twenty20 in South Africa, but the young opener showed his immense promise before the tournament with a fine 81 against Pakistan.
Shakib Al Hasan: A highly economical slow left-arm bowler and more than capable with the bat, Shakib Al Hasan will fill one of Bangladesh's all-rounder spots.

The Main Contenders: Pakistan (Group B)

Pakistan had a torrid and traumatic time of things at the 2007 World Cup in the Caribbean. They suffered a tournament-ending shock defeat to Ireland and were then forced to mourn the mysterious death of their coach, Bob Woolmer. The side was in turmoil, but the ICC World Twenty20 tournament in South Africa, six months after the horrors of the World Cup, offered Pakistan cricket a chance for redemption.

Misbah-ul-Haq: The advent of Twenty20 cricket has revitalized his international career.

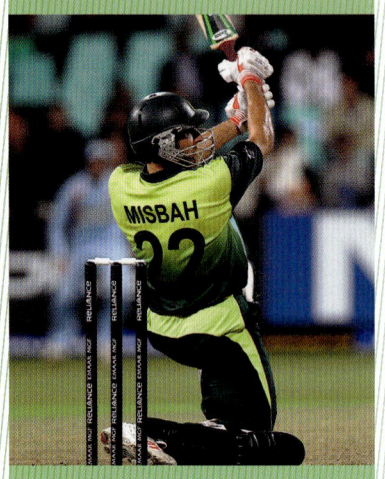

Coach: Geoff Lawson
Captain: Shoaib Malik
Matches: P12, W9, L2, Tied 1, NR 0
Win percentage: 0.750
Highest total: 203 for 5, v Bangladesh at Karachi, 20 April 2008
Lowest total: 129 for 8, v South Africa at Johannesburg, 2 February 2007
Most runs: Misbah-ul-Haq (338)
Highest score: 87 not out – Misbah-ul-Haq, v Bangladesh at Karachi, 20 April 2008
Most wickets: Shahid Afridi (15)
Best bowling: 4 for 18 – Mohammad Asif, v India at Durban, 14 September 2007
Best economy rate (qualification: four wickets): Umar Gul (5.37)
2007 T20 World Cup performance: Runners-up

The Pakistan selectors understandably saw the competition as a chance to introduce a few fresh faces into the squad, but their selection still raised a few eyebrows. Mohammad Yousuf – prolific in all forms of cricket in previous years – and the experienced Abdul Razzaq were omitted; included was Misbah-ul-Haq, a player who had been languishing in the international wilderness for three years but who had shone in domestic Twenty20 cricket.

Preparations, however, were far from ideal. Just days before the start of the tournament, news emerged of a dressing-room spat between Shoaib Akhtar and Mohammad Asif. Shoaib was sent packing in disgrace; 22-year-old Sohail Tanvir was called up to replace him; and a sense of unease hovered over the Pakistan squad. Would they be better off without the notoriously disruptive influence of Shoaib Akhtar in their squad?

Scotland may not be the best barometer of a team's standing in world cricket, but a 51-run victory would have done much to ease any Pakistani nerves. What's more, the win handed Pakistan an opportunity to knock their next group opponents, arch-rivals India, out of the competition. Things did not work out like that, but the two rivals served up a feast of cricket. Mohammad Asif put behind him any problems he may have experienced following his bust-up with Shoaib Akhtar to take 4 for 18 and Misbah-ul-Haq did much to silence the critics with 53 as the match ended in a thrilling tie.

The result gave the Pakistan squad huge belief. Captain Shoaib Malik (57) and Younis Khan (51) – the man who had turned down the chance to captain his country following the World Cup – took Pakistan to a challenging 189 for 6 en route to a 33-run victory over Sri Lanka. However, it was only after they had produced a controlled and clinical performance to beat Australia by six wickets in their following match – a result that put them on the brink of a semi-final place – that commentators started to talk up Pakistan's chances of winning the competition.

The dream continued. A whirlwind 39 off 15 balls from Shahid Afridi at the top of the order handed Pakistan a six-wicket victory over Bangladesh. In the semi-final, the Pakistan bowlers, led by the excellent Umar Gul (3 for 15), made light of Shoaib Akhtar's absence by restricting New Zealand to 143 for 8. Imran Nazir made a quickfire 59 at the top of the order and Pakistan made it home with seven balls to spare. They had made it through to the final.

And that is where the dream turned sour: a fantastic spectacle the World Twenty20 final may have been, but a moment of misjudgement from Misbah-ul-Haq, who had been ice-cool in his single-handed attempt to drag his side over the finishing line, ultimately cost them the match, and Pakistan were forced to look on as India celebrated a five-run victory in front of the world's media. The core of the squad remains for 2009. This time round, though, nothing short of victory will suffice.

Looking to leap the final hurdle

Shahid Afridi: His all-action style is a perfect fit for Twenty20 cricket.

STAR PLAYER:
Shahid Afridi
Born: 1 March 1980, Khyber Agency, Pakistan
Matches: 11 **Innings:** 10 **Runs:** 168 **Ave:** 16.80
Scoring rate: 169.69
Wickets: 15 **Runs:** 280 **Ave:** 18.66 **Economy rate:** 6.74
Highest score: 39 (v Bangladesh at Cape Town, 20 September 2007)
Best bowling: 4 for 19 (v Scotland at Durban, 12 September 2007)

Now one of the senior players in the Pakistan squad, Shahid Afridi made the headlines back in 1996 when, aged 16, he scored the fastest century in one-day international history (102 off 40 balls) on his debut against Sri Lanka. A whirling dervish with the bat, he also has a bag of tricks at his disposal with the ball and has matured over the years into one of the most destructive players in the business. He ended the 2007 World Twenty20 as player of the tournament and will have to be at his best if Pakistan are to shine in England in 2009.

SUPPORTING CAST
Misbah-ul-Haq: More than justified his controversial selection ahead of the prolific Mohammad Yousuf for the 2007 World Twenty20 by ending the tournament as Pakistan's best batsman.
Shoaib Malik: Handed the captaincy after Pakistan's disastrous 2007 50-over World Cup campaign, the batting all-rounder has proved an inspired choice as captain.
Shoaib Akhtar: Controversial and disruptive he may be, but there are few finer sights in world cricket than the Rawalpindi Express steaming to the crease with the ball in his hand.
Umar Gul: Made the most of his exceptional control and ability with the ball to hit the seam to end the 2007 World Twenty20 as the tournament's leading wicket-taker with 13 wickets.
Younis Khan: The best Pakistan batsman of his generation in all forms of the game, Younis Khan provides his side with a rich seam of runs in the middle order.

The Main Contenders: England (Group B)

England started their international T20 campaign in June 2005 like a cork shooting out of a champagne bottle. They hammered Australia and went on to produce a summer of electrifying cricket that culminated in a first Ashes win in 18 years. But England's performances in the T20 arena since that morale-boosting summer day – like their cricket in all formats of the game – have gone disappointingly flat.

Andrew Flintoff: After months of injury hell, the talismanic all-rounder looks to be firing on all cylinders again.

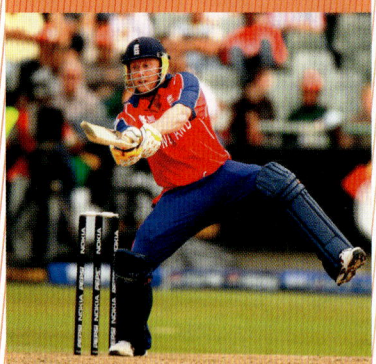

Coach: Vacant
Captain: Andrew Strauss
Matches: P14, W6, L8, Tied 0
Win percentage: 0.429
Highest total: 200 for 6, v India at Durban, 19 September 2007
Lowest total: 99 all out, v Stanford Superstars, 1 November 2008, Antigua
Most runs: Kevin Pietersen (363)
Highest score: 79 – Paul Collingwood, v West Indies at The Oval, 28 June 2007; Kevin Pietersen, v Zimbabwe at Cape Town, 13 September 2007
Most wickets: 13 – Paul Collingwood, Stuart Broad
Best bowling: 4 for 22 – Paul Collingwood, v Sri Lanka at Southampton, 15 June 2006
Best economy rate (qualification: four wickets): 6.44 – Andrew Flintoff
2007 T20 World Cup performance: Super Eights

Twenty20 cricket was a different animal back in 2005. Australia were not as pumped up for the "novelty" game as their English counterparts who, inspired by a partisan and boisterous crowd and fuelled by months of pre-Ashes media hype, produced a stunning performance to win by 100 runs. The good news was that the match inflicted a psychological blow on the Australians that lasted the duration of the summer; the bad news was that the Rose Bowl massacre remains England's best T20 performance to this day.

A year passed before England re-entered the T20 fray. They bowled out Sri Lanka for 163, again at the Rose Bowl, but fell a disappointing three runs short of the target. A pattern was set. Over the next 18 months, successive defeats against Pakistan, Australia and the West Indies (twice) – including a series of poor displays in the 50-over World Cup – provided England with scant preparation for the inaugural ICC Twenty20 World Cup in September 2007. They travelled to South Africa with few backers and their performances did little to satisfy the sceptics.

England used more personnel during the course of the tournament (15) than any of the other Test-playing nations. Players who had enjoyed domestic T20 success – such as Darren Maddy, Chris Schofield and Jeremy Snape – were thrown into the international fray in a desperate attempt to end the losing streak. Things started well with an opening 50-run win over Zimbabwe, but any dreams of glory were short-lived.

Next up were Australia, and the recently crowned 50-over world champions were in no mood for a repeat of the Rose Bowl debacle. They chased down England's disappointing total of 135 with an embarrassing five overs to spare. England's T20 World Cup blushes did not end there. They lost to South Africa (by 19 runs), and then to New Zealand (by 5 runs), but the worst was still to come. England found themselves on the wrong end of an Indian mauling, with Yuvraj Singh crashing Stuart Broad for six sixes in an over as the Indians posted a mighty 214 for 4. England saved some face by reaching 200 for 6, but their fourth straight defeat sent them crashing limply out of the tournament.

The road to recovery started in New Zealand in February 2008. Back-to-back victories over the Black Caps signalled an end to the pick-and-mix selection policy that had so seriously undermined their World Cup chances. Ian Bell, Ravi Bopara and Owais Shah have added ballast to a batting line-up dominated by the destructive Kevin Pietersen and Paul Collingwood. Steve Harmison, Broad, James Anderson and a fit-again Andrew Flintoff form the core of a bowling attack capable of stifling any international batsman. The side still has its doubters, only increased by the Stanford Series debacle, but the squad possesses the ingredients for success.

For their fans that moment cannot come quickly enough. The champagne days of the summer of 2005 are starting to feel like a distant memory.

Still finding their Twenty20 feet

Kevin Pietersen: The hugely talented stroke-maker poses England's biggest threat with the bat.

STAR PLAYER:
Kevin Pietersen
Born: 27 June 1980, Pietermaritzburg, South Africa
Matches: 14 **Innings:** 14 **Runs:** 363 **Ave:** 27.92
Scoring rate: 148.77
Highest score: 79 (v Zimbabwe at Cape Town, 13 September 2007)

Not since the days when Viv Richards was in his prime has international cricket seen such swagger. Since making his debut for England in 2005, South African-born Kevin Pietersen's uncomplicated but unorthodox approach to power hitting has made him one of the biggest draws in the game. Exceptional in both Test and one-day cricket, the former England captain has yet to truly find his feet in the T20 arena, but a big score is just around the corner for a player of such talent. It will be an innings any cricket fan around the world would pay good money to go and see.

SUPPORTING CAST
Ian Bell: Seems to have found a home at the top of the order. Possesses great technique and timing and in full flow is England's most pleasing batsman on the eye.
Stuart Broad: Useful with both bat and ball and came to the fore with some outstanding performances on domestic Twenty20 competition. He is England's most exciting prospect.
Paul Collingwood: The experienced all-rounder and former captain has found form hard to come by in recent times, but brings a wealth of experience to the side.
Andrew Flintoff: Has struggled with injuries in recent times, but is as miserly as they come with the ball and the big man is still capable of destruction with the bat.
Steve Harmison: Arrived back in the England side with a bang after a spell on the fringes and brings hostility to the new-ball attack.

The Main Contenders: Australia (Group C)

It may have been due to the late start of a domestic Twenty20 league in Australia (the first competition was staged there in 2005–06) or down to the fact that their international T20 experience was limited to one-off games aimed mostly at promoting an upcoming Test series, but it took some time for Australia to see the 20-over format game as anything other than a novelty.

Andrew Symonds: On his day, the most destructive batsman in world cricket.

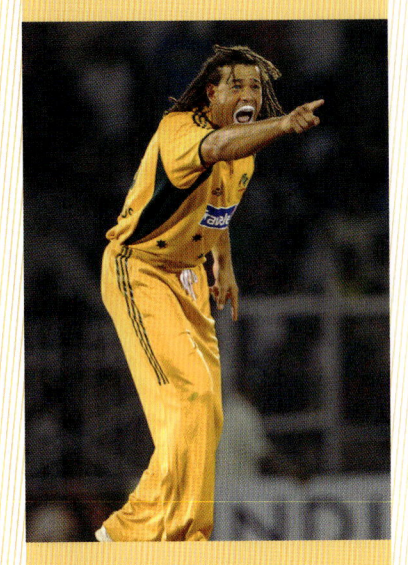

Captain: Ricky Ponting
Matches: P15, W8, L7, Tied 0
Win percentage: 0.533
Highest total: 221 for 5, v England at Sydney, 9 January 2007
Lowest total: 79, v England at Southampton, 13 June 2005
Most runs: 337 – Andrew Symonds
Highest score: 98 not out – Ricky Ponting, v New Zealand at Auckland, 17 February 2005
Most wickets: 15 – Nathan Bracken
Best bowling: 4 for 20 – Stuart Clark, v Sri Lanka at Cape Town, 20 September 2007
Best economy rate (qualification: four wickets): 5.46 – Ashley Noffke
2007 T20 World Cup performance: Semi-finals

Australia had featured in the first-ever Twenty20 international (a crushing 44-run victory over New Zealand in Auckland). They had been on the receiving end of a 100-run defeat by a pumped-up England prior to the start of the 2005 Ashes series, had shared a win and a defeat against South Africa and had crushed an England side still reeling from a sorry defence of their Ashes in January 2007. But when Australia arrived in South Africa for the start of the World Twenty20 in September 2007, they had not played a game in anger since retaining their 50-over World Cup crown in the Caribbean five months earlier. They were under-prepared and, in their opening game against Zimbabwe whose standing in international cricket had perhaps never been lower, it was all too evident.

If anyone was to blame it was the batsmen. Australia limped to 138 for 9; Zimbabwe, led by a battling, unbeaten 60 from Brendan Taylor, passed the total with one ball to spare to secure arguably the greatest win in their history. For Australia the equation was simple: they had to beat England to stay in the competition.

But Australia are notoriously at their most dangerous when wounded, and England were the first to feel the backlash. Impressive bowling from Nathan Bracken (3 for 16) and Mitchell Johnson (3 for 22) restricted England to 135 all out before Matthew Hayden (67 not out) and Adam Gilchrist (45) led them to an eight-wicket victory. Given the recent context of international cricket, everyone assumed it would be business as usual for Australia – a feeling confirmed after Hayden (73 not out) and Gilchrist (43) fired them to a comfortable nine-wicket win over Bangladesh.

But then the chinks in Australia's armour were laid bare once again. For once the openers misfired, Australia reached 164 for 7 and Pakistan, showing a consistency and control normally associated with their opponents, eased past the total with five balls and six wickets in hand. The stop-start campaign continued with a ten-wicket demolition of Sri Lanka (a game that saw Brett Lee record the first hat-trick in international T20 history). But then their momentum came to a crunching halt in the semi-final against India.

A total of 189 was always going to be a tough target for the Australians, but when Hayden (62) and Andrew Symonds (45) were at the crease, hope remained that they could sneak past the winning post. Instead, India's fairy-tale continued, Australia fell short by 15 runs and had failed to make the final of a major international competition for the first time since the 2004 Champions Trophy in England.

Australia's build-up to the 2009 tournament has been patchy (a pair of wins and a defeat against India, a victory over New Zealand and a loss to the West Indies), but the rise of the domestic Twenty20 tournament in Australia, coupled with the mass exodus of players to the Indian Premier League, has enabled Australia to review a greater number of players. When they finally hit upon the right formula, Australia are sure to fire.

Out to prove a serious point

Brett Lee: The spearhead of the Australian attack is no longer just about pace.

STAR PLAYER:
Brett Lee
Born: 8 November 1976, Wollongong, New South Wales, Australia
Matches: 13 **Innings:** 6 **Runs:** 75 **Ave:** 25.00 **Scoring rate:** 138.88
Wickets: 12 **Runs:** 334 **Ave:** 27.83 **Economy rate:** 7.23
Highest score: 43 not out (v South Africa at Johannesburg, 24 February 2006)
Best bowling: 3 for 27 (v Bangladesh at Cape Town, 16 September 2007)

The spearhead and senior partner of the Australian attack following the retirement of Shane Warne and Glenn McGrath, Brett Lee seems to have got over his injury-riddled days when speed was everything and appears to have added more variety to the bouncer/yorker routines of yesteryear. Not that this has detracted from his destructive wicket-taking abilities: at the 2007 World Twenty20 against Bangladesh, he became the first bowler to take a hat-trick in a T20 international match. The pin-up boy of Australian cricket will have to be at his best in England in 2009 if his side are to add the Twenty20 world championship to their impressive haul of trophies.

SUPPORTING CAST
Stuart Clark: Charged with filling the huge void left by the retirement of pace ace Glenn McGrath, Stuart Clark ended the 2007 World Twenty20 as Australia's leading wicket-taker and most economical bowler.
Matthew Hayden: The veteran opener may be in the twilight of his career, but he continues to churn out the runs at the top of the Australian order.
Ricky Ponting: Australia's best batsman, the Tasmanian leads from the front. He will be keen to put the disappointments of South Africa 2007 behind him.
Andrew Symonds: A destructive presence with the bat and increasingly influential with the ball; any side in the world would want Symonds in their T20 side – as proved by the US$1.35 million IPL outfit Deccan Chargers paid for his services in 2007.
Shane Watson: Showed his aptitude for the 20-over game with some stunning performances with both bat and ball for the Rajasthan Royals in the 2008 Indian Premier League. A shoo-in to the Australian squad if he can stay fit.

The Main Contenders: Sri Lanka (Group C)

Of all the Test-playing countries, Sri Lanka perhaps paid the greatest price for Twenty20's lowly standing in its formative years, in the days when a 20-over international was viewed as little more than an unwanted addition to an already over-packed international schedule. By the time the team arrived for the start of the World Twenty20, they had competed in a mere three T20 internationals.

Muttiah Muralitharan: The leading wicket-taker in Test cricket will be keen to shine after missing out in 2007.

Coach: Trevor Bayliss
Captain: Mahela Jayawardene
Matches: P8, W5, L3, Tied 0
Win percentage: 0.625
Highest total: 260 for 6, v Kenya at Johannesburg, 14 September 2007
Lowest total: 101, v Australia at Cape Town, 20 September 2007
Most runs: 246 – Sanath Jayasuriya
Highest score: 88 – Sanath Jayasuriya, v Kenya at Johannesburg, 14 September 2007
Most wickets: 10 – Dilhara Fernando
Best bowling: 3 for 19 – Dilhara Fernando, v New Zealand at Auckland, 26 December 2006
Best economy rate (qualification: four wickets):
5.81 – Chaminda Vaas
2007 T20 World Cup performance: Super Eights

Sri Lanka arrived in South Africa bolstered by their performances in the 50-over World Cup in the Caribbean a few months earlier, when they had rolled back the years with some scintillating performances to reach the final, only to lose to Australia. They had every reason to believe they could succeed in the 20-over game and, because of their attacking style of cricket, many commentators considered them the tournament's dark horses.

Then came the bad news. Word filtered through from England that Muttiah Muralitharan, the leading wicket-taker in Test history and Sri Lanka's deadliest bowler, had injured his elbow while on domestic duty for Lancashire and would miss the tournament. It must have come as a bitter blow for Sri Lankan hopes.

Not that they showed it in their opening encounter with Kenya, a match that saw them get off to a record-breaking start. Veteran opener Sanath Jayasuriya smashed 88 off 44 balls, captain Mahela Jayawardene chipped in with 65 and Jehan Mubarak's late fireworks (46 off 13 balls) propelled Sri Lanka to a world-record total of 260 for 6. It left Kenya with a mountain they were never likely to climb. Demoralized, they slumped to a meagre 88 all out.

With Jayasuriya (61) to the fore once again, Sri Lanka's good form continued with a comfortable seven-wicket win over New Zealand. They had got off to the perfect start, and were more than living up to their pre-tournament "dark horse" billing. But then the wheels started to fall off their World Twenty20 campaign.

Pakistan were simply too good for them, notching up a challenging total of 189 for 6. In reply, Sri Lanka failed to recover from the loss of Upul Tharanga and Jayasuriya in the space of the first seven balls, slumped to 115 for 7 and finished on 156 for 9 – a dispiriting 33 runs short of the target. The next match, against Bangladesh, should have been a comfortable prelude to a winner-takes-all clash against Australia, and although Sri Lanka won it, the 64-run margin of victory could do little to hide Sri Lanka's problems with the bat. They had laboured to 147 for 5 and had been rescued by their bowlers. Jayasuriya had failed twice in succession, and without his runs the team had been unable to build decent totals. They had escaped against Bangladesh; the lingering sentiment was that Australia would surely not be as forgiving.

The writing was on the wall from the moment Jayasuriya succumbed leg before to Brett Lee for his third consecutive duck. This time, Sri Lanka paid the ultimate price for their failure to build a total without their veteran talisman's runs, being dismissed for a disappointing total of 101. Australia, led by Matthew Hayden (58 not out) and Adam Gilchrist (31 not out) made short work of Sri Lanka's bowlers, cruising to the target in just 10.1 overs and dumping Sri Lanka out of the tournament in emphatic fashion.

Success at international T20 cricket may still be elusive for Sri Lanka, but a domestic league is now in place and most of the international players are involved in the Indian Premier League.

Dangerous in any form of limited-overs cricket

STAR PLAYER:
Sanath Jayasuriya
Born: 30 June 1969, Matara, Sri Lanka
Matches: 7 **Innings:** 7 **Runs:** 246 **Ave:** 41.00
Scoring rate: 165.10
Wickets: 9 **Runs:** 155 **Ave:** 17.22 **Economy rate:** 7.44
Highest score: 88 (v Kenya at Johannesburg, 14 September 2007)
Best bowling: 3 for 21 (v New Zealand at Wellington, 22 December 2006)

Such is his importance to the Sri Lankan team that when Sanath Jayasuriya, fast approaching his 39th birthday, was omitted from Sri Lanka's one-day squad to face the West Indies in March 2008, the country's sports minister intervened to demand his inclusion. Despite the years, the veteran opener remains a prolific free-flowing batsman with magnificent ball-striking abilities. He played two mesmerizing knocks during Sri Lanka's 2007 World Twenty20 campaign and was a stand-out performer with the Mumbai Indians in the IPL. If the 2009 tournament in England is to be Jayasuriya's international swansong, you can be sure he will want to go out in style.

SUPPORTING CAST
Mahela Jayawardene: Has responded to the task of captaining his country side in style. A fine technician with the bat, he was Sri Lanka's leading run-scorer in South Africa in 2007.
Ajantha Mendis: The leg-spinner burst on to the international scene in 2008 with some record-breaking performances in the Test series against India.
Muttiah Muralitharan: The world's leading Test wicket-taker missed the 2007 World Twenty20 tournament through injury. He will be keen to stamp his mark on the 2009 tournament.
Kumar Sangakkara: Arguably the best wicketkeeper-batsman in world cricket. The graceful left-hander's runs will be crucial to the Sri Lankan cause.
Chaminda Vaas: Steady as ever with the ball, the veteran left-arm pace bowler topped the economy rate tables for Sri Lanka in 2007, going for a miserly 5.55 runs per over.

Sanath Jayasuriya: The 20-over format has enabled the veteran opener to roll back the years.

The Main Contenders: West Indies (Group C)

These are tough times for West Indian cricket. Money to develop the game is scarce, results in all forms of the game have been indifferent, and a new generation of players continue to struggle against feverish expectations raised by the performances of West Indian legends from yesteryear. And if anyone thought the 20-over format of the game would provide the West Indies with some relief, they were sadly mistaken.

Dwayne Bravo: The Trinidad native is the most talented all-rounder to emerge from the Caribbean for years.

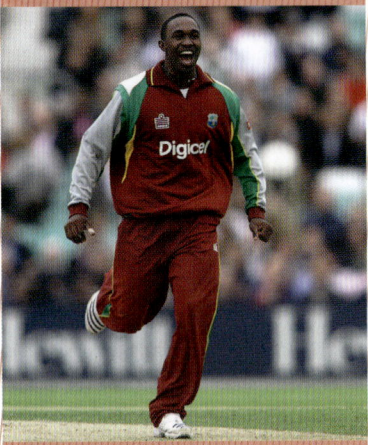

Coach: John Dyson
Captain: Chris Gayle
Matches: P8, W3, L4, Tied 1
Win percentage: 0.375
Highest total: 208 for 8, v England at The Oval, 28 June 2007
Lowest total: 126 for 7, v New Zealand at Auckland, 16 February 2007
Most runs: 193 – Chris Gayle
Highest score: 117 – Chris Gayle, v South Africa at Johannesburg, 11 September 2007
Most wickets: 7 – Jerome Taylor, Darren Sammy
Best bowling: 3 for 6 – Jerome Taylor, v South Africa at Port Elizabeth, 16 December 2007
Best economy rate (qualification: four wickets): 6.71 – Darren Sammy
2007 T20 World Cup performance: Group stage

Not that it all started so badly. The West Indies played out a tie with New Zealand in February 2006 – a game noted more for Chris Cairns' curtain call to the international game than for the quality of cricket on display – and then went on to outperform England in every department in the first of two matches played at The Oval in June 2007. They won the match by 15 runs after posting a mammoth total of 208 for 8, although England came much closer to the target than perhaps they should have.

The following day showed the first sign of weakness in the West Indies game. Led by a fine 61 by Chris Gayle, they reached a respectable 161 for 9 and had England on the ropes at 104 for 5 in the 14th over, until Owais Shah (55 not out) caressed the West Indian bowlers around the vast Oval outfield to lead his side to an unlikely five-wicket victory.

Then came the World Twenty20 in South Africa and the West Indies kicked off their campaign in spectacular fashion. Yet another mesmerizing performance from Gayle with the bat – he smashed a magnificent 57-ball 117 (the first century in T20 international history) – led them to an imposing total of 205 for 6 that should have put the game beyond South Africa's reach. But, well as Gayle performed with the bat, his team-mates were woeful both with the ball and in the field. Three dropped catches and a record-breaking 23 wides tell their own story; helped by a savage 55-ball 90 from Herschelle Gibbs, South Africa romped to the mighty target with eight wickets and 2.2 overs in hand. The islanders had played only one match and already they found themselves on the back foot.

It was a case of déjà vu two days later against Bangladesh. Gayle may have failed on this occasion – falling for a third-ball duck – but a 94-run partnership between Devon Smith and Shivnarine Chanderpaul, coupled with some late cameos from Marlon Samuels and Dwayne Smith, hoisted the West Indies to a respectable 164 for 8. In reply, Bangladesh captain Mohammad Ashraful (dropped by Fidel Edwards on 29) blasted the fastest half-century in T20 international history and, supported by Aftab Ahmed (62 not out), carried his team over the finishing line with two full overs to spare and four wickets in hand. The West Indies' tournament was over before it had the chance to get started, and back in the islands the recriminations were about to do their usual rounds

Former captain Garfield Sobers claimed that "something very drastic" had to be done; captain Ramnaresh Sarwan bemoaned his side's deficiencies in the field; the players' attitude towards the game was brought into question. But West Indian cricket fans have heard all of these arguments before. The West Indies possess a talented – and, following their success in the Stanford Twenty20 Challenge, considerably richer – group of players, but the South Africa debacle has left them in a tough group alongside Australia and Sri Lanka and they must beat at least one of those teams to improve on their dismal performance at the 2007 World Twenty20. It is hard to see them doing that.

On the road to nowhere fast

Chris Gayle: The West Indies captain leads from the front, often in spell-binding fashion.

STAR PLAYER:
Chris Gayle
Born: 21 September 1979, Kingston, Jamaica
Matches: 5 **Innings:** 5 **Runs:** 193 **Ave:** 38.60
Scoring rate: 164.95
Highest score: 117 (v South Africa at Johannesburg, 11 September 2007)

Tall and imposing at the crease, Chris Gayle has been one of the few shining lights in an otherwise unprecedented period of gloom for West Indies cricket. His team may have failed in South Africa in 2007, but Gayle emerged as one of the stars of the tournament, cracking a mesmerizing 57-ball 117 against the host nation in the opening game. He missed out on the 2007 IPL season with a groin injury, but will be keen to use the 2009 World Twenty20 to reaffirm his status as one of the leading T20 players in the game.

SUPPORTING CAST
Dwayne Bravo: A useful middle-order batsman and an effective swing bowler, the Trinidad all-rounder is one of the most exciting prospects to have emerged from the Caribbean in years.
Shivnarine Chanderpaul: So often the glue that holds the West Indies innings together, the veteran left-hander is a vital cog in his country's batting line-up.
Fidel Edwards: The Barbados fast bowler adds genuine pace to the West Indies attack and his ability to reverse-swing the ball makes him an effective death bowler.
Ramnaresh Sarwan: Having lost out to Gayle in the battle for the West Indies captaincy, the Guyana right-hander will be out to prove a point with the bat.
Jerome Taylor: The spearhead of the West Indies pace attack. Fast and accurate with the ball, when he is free from injury the Jamaican is a potential match-winner.

The Main Contenders: New Zealand (Group D)

New Zealand may have been among the first to embrace Twenty20 at international level – they played in and hosted the first-ever international (against Australia) and in the first on South African soil – but waited until the 2006–07 season before hosting a domestic league. As such the Black Caps, like many of the teams, travelled to the 2007 World Twenty20 with little idea of where they stood in the 20-over format of the game.

Jacob Oram: There are few harder-hitting batsmen in world cricket than the 1.98m all-rounder.

Coach: Andy Moles
Captain: Daniel Vettori
Matches: P16, W5, L10, Tied 1
Win percentage: 0.313
Highest total: 190, v India at Johannesburg, 16 September 2007
Lowest total: 123 for 9, v England at Manchester, 13 June 2008
Most runs: 323 – Brendon McCullum
Highest score: 66 not out – Jacob Oram, v Australia at Perth, 11 December 2007
Most wickets: 13 – Daniel Vettori
Best bowling: 4 for 7 – Mark Gillespie, v Kenya at Durban, 12 September 2007
Best economy rate (qualification: four wickets): 5.63 – Daniel Vettori
2007 T20 World Cup performance: Semi-finals

A relatively successful 50-over World Cup campaign in the Caribbean four months earlier would have seen them travel to South Africa in a confident mood, but also one intent on revenge. The Black Caps' defeat to Sri Lanka in the semi-final had done little to dispel the team's chokers tag. It was the fifth time New Zealand had lost in the semi-finals of a major tournament – and the wait for a shot at one of the game's major prizes went on.

It was all change at the top, too. Long-standing captain Stephen Fleming stood down following the Sri Lanka defeat, with veteran spinner Daniel Vettori named his successor, and to signal the start of the new era, Fleming was omitted from the New Zealand squad to allow the new man complete freedom to stamp his mark on the team.

They got off to a convincing start, making light work of Kenya, dismissing them for 73 – the lowest-ever score in international T20 cricket – and breezing past the total in a mere 7.4 overs. Sri Lanka lay ahead and, although the match may have been a dead rubber, it provided the Black Caps with a chance to avenge the last-four defeat in the Caribbean. A swashbuckling 62 from Ross Taylor helped New Zealand to 164 for 7, but then Sanath Jayasuriya set to work. The veteran opener's innings was far from chanceless (he was dropped twice), but a 44-ball 61 did much to push Sri Lanka to victory with seven balls to spare. The chance for revenge had passed New Zealand by and they knew there was plenty of room for improvement.

Vettori led from the front as the Black Caps kicked off their Super Eights campaign with a morale-boosting ten-run victory over India. They made it two wins in two with a narrow five-run win over England in Cape Town two days later. The victory secured them a spot in the final four. First, though, they had a match-up against South Africa in Durban. They lost by six wickets. The result may not have mattered, but a six-wicket defeat was hardly the ideal preparation for a semi-final showdown against an in-form Pakistan team that was firing on all cylinders.

Openers Brendon McCullum and Lou Vincent produced a 50-run opening stand and provided the Black Caps with a solid base from which to launch an assault on a target approaching 180. But then they started to unravel: Umar Gul took 3 for 15; New Zealand slipped to 143 for 8; Pakistan staggered over the finishing line off the final ball of their innings; and New Zealand – doing little to shake off the "chokers" tag that so irritates them – had once again stumbled at the semi-final stage.

Things have not improved for New Zealand. Events in South Africa seem to have knocked the wind out of their Twenty20 sails; they followed the tournament with defeats to Australia, South Africa and England (three times). With the careers of many of the older "golden" generation coming to an end, New Zealand have some distance to travel on their way to finding a solution to unlocking the door to the prize-winning moments of major tournaments.

On the cusp of international glory

Daniel Vettori: The veteran has shone with the ball since taking over the New Zealand captaincy in 2007.

STAR PLAYER:
Daniel Vettori
Born: 27 January 1979, Auckland, New Zealand
Matches: 9 **Wickets:** 13 **Runs:** 203 **Ave:** 15.61
Economy rate: 5.63
Best bowling: 4 for 20 (v India at Johannesburg, 16 September 2007)

Daniel Vettori seems to have grown in stature since taking over the New Zealand captaincy following Stephen Fleming's long reign. The leading left-arm spinner in world cricket, he showed his mastery of the art at the 2007 ICC World Twenty20 – his first tournament in charge of the Black Caps. He guided his side to the semi-finals, took 11 wickets and topped the tournament's economy rate charts after conceding a miserly 5.33 runs per over. Also a more than capable performer with the bat, Vettori has to fire if New Zealand are to break their major tournament duck in 2009.

SUPPORTING CAST

Brendon McCullum: A potentially destructive presence at the top of the New Zealand order, as shown by his world-record-breaking knock of 158 for Kolkata in the 2007 IPL.

Jacob Oram: A hard-hitting batsman and an effective medium-pace bowler, Oram was one of five New Zealand players to feature in the inaugural IPL season. The all-rounder has gained vital experience in 20-over cricket.

Jesse Ryder: Attracted headlines for all the wrong reasons in 2008 after damaging his hand in a nightclub. This talented batsman will be keen to shine at the 2009 ICC World Twenty20.

Scott Styris: Has a wealth of experience following stints in English county cricket and the IPL. He retired from Test cricket in 2008 to prolong his career in limited-overs formats of the game.

Ross Taylor: A solid tournament at the 2009 World Twenty20 will confirm the hard-hitting, free-scoring Wellington player's reputation as the leading light in New Zealand's batting line-up.

The Main Contenders: South Africa (Group D)

In recent years, South Africa have quietly risen up the world rankings to as high as No.2 in both the Test and 50-over formats of the game. If they want to take over Australia's mantle as the strongest cricketing nation on the planet, though, trophies in the major international competitions are going to have to start coming their way. Don't be surprised if they get that particular ball rolling at the 2009 ICC World Twenty20.

Dale Steyn: The spearhead of the South Africa attack needs to add more than just pace to his armoury.

Coach: Mickey Arthur
Captain: Graeme Smith
Matches: P13, W8, L5, Tied 0
Win percentage: 0.615
Highest total: 208 for 2, v West Indies at Johannesburg, 11 September 2007
Lowest total: 114, v Australia at Brisbane, 9 January 2006
Most runs: 364 – Graeme Smith
Highest score: 90 not out – Herschelle Gibbs, v West Indies at Johannesburg, 11 September 2007
Most wickets: 15 – Shaun Pollock
Best bowling: 4 for 9 – Dale Steyn, v West Indies at Port Elizabeth, 16 December 2007
Best economy rate (qualification: four wickets): 3.71 – Dale Steyn
2007 T20 World Cup performance: Super Eights

Hopes had been high going into the 2007 ICC World Twenty20. South Africa were hosting the tournament – and so could enjoy the lion's share of the support – and the team had also enjoyed a fairly decent record in the shortened format of the game. They could point to considerable firepower in the batting ranks, with Graeme Smith, Herschelle Gibbs, Justin Kemp, Luke Bosman, Mark Boucher and Albie Morkel all more than capable of destroying an opposition attack. They had an array of fast bowlers at their disposal as well – including Dale Steyn and Morne Morkel – but if there was a weakness, it was the lack of personnel capable of bowling at the death. South Africa's critics were convinced this would count against them at some stage in the tournament.

And for 16.2 overs of South Africa's opening match against the West Indies, it seemed the critics were right. Chris Gayle despatched the home attack to all corners of the Johannesburg Bullring en route to the first century in international T20 history as the West Indies amassed what should have been a match-winning total of 205 for 6. But then Gibbs produced some fireworks of his own, carving out an unbeaten 55-ball 90 to hand his side a winning start to the tournament, if not an altogether convincing one. A more comfortable seven-wicket victory over Bangladesh set them up nicely for the second stage.

A murderous knock of 43 from 20 balls from Albie Morkel and an inspirational spell of bowling from Shaun Pollock – the veteran pace bowler conceded just 17 runs, including one boundary, from his four overs – saw South Africa to a comfortable 19-run win over England. And when they cruised to victory over New Zealand – with Morne Morkel (4 for 17) and Kemp (89 not out) the heroes of the hour – people started to talk up South Africa's chances of winning the tournament. To secure a semi-final spot, all they had to do was avoid a heavy defeat against India.

They were the unbeaten team remaining in the tournament and, on the bowler-friendly Durban pitch, entered the match as strong favourites. India recovered from 33 for 3 to record a respectable 153 for 5. Taking into account various run-rate permutations, South Africa only needed to make 126 to join India in the semi-finals. They imploded. RP Singh and Sreesanth ripped through South Africa's top order, reducing the home side to 31 for 5 in the fifth over. They mustered a recovery of sorts, but fell some 37 runs short of the target. The dream was over as the massed ranks of fans filed home disappointed. But the recriminations had barely started.

The word "chokers" was bandied around in some quarters. After all, this was not the first time South Africa had suffered an ignominious exit from a major tournament. But the doom-mongers missed the point. Bar the defeat against India, South Africa had enjoyed a highly creditable campaign and with the majority of their star players having gained added experience of the 20-over game in the Indian Premier League, they have the required armoury to go all the way in England in 2009.

On the hunt for major honours

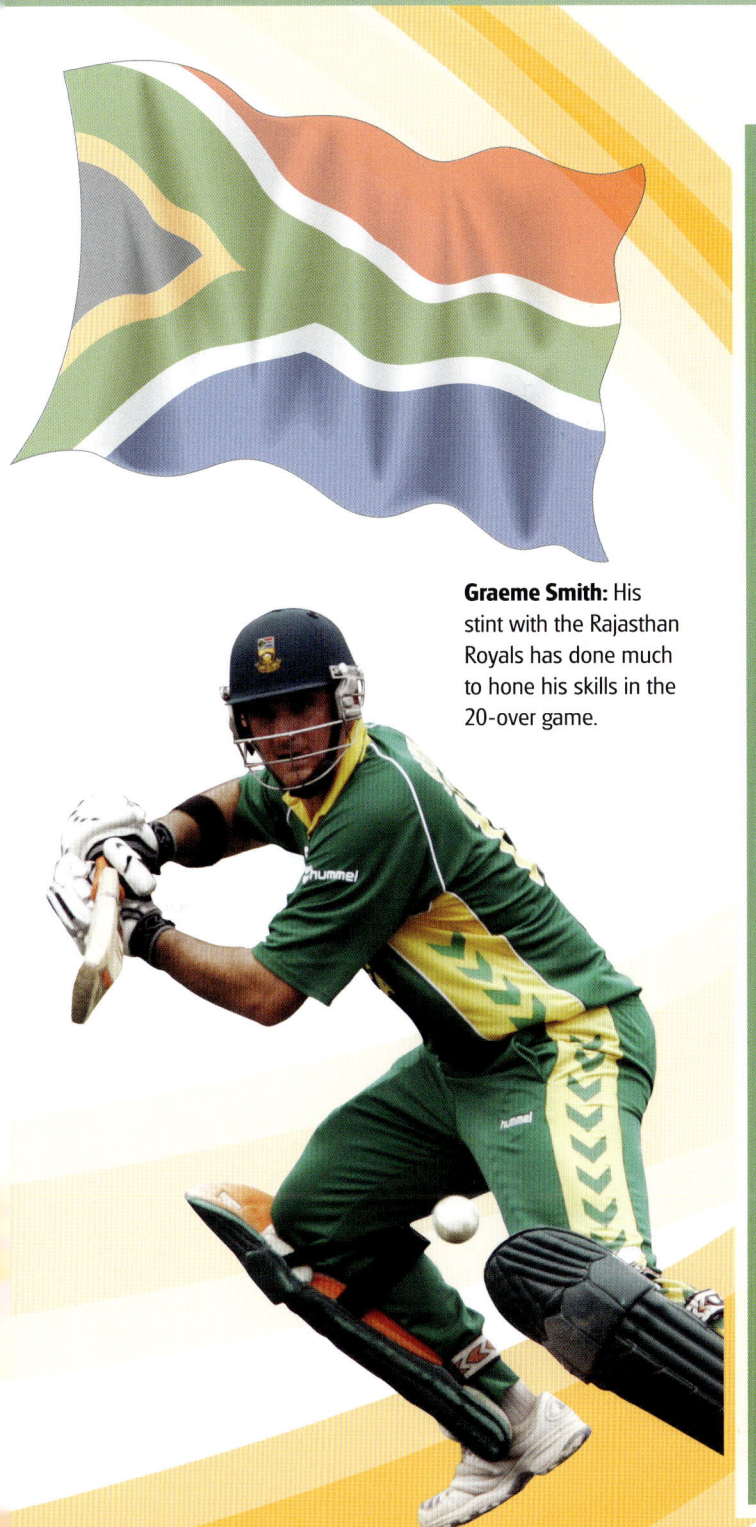

Graeme Smith: His stint with the Rajasthan Royals has done much to hone his skills in the 20-over game.

STAR PLAYER:
Graeme Smith
Born: 1 February 1981, Johannesburg, South Africa
Matches: 12 **Innings:** 12 **Runs:** 364 **Ave:** 36.40
Scoring rate: 127.27
Highest score: 89 not out (v Australia at Johannesburg, 24 February 2006)

Graeme Smith has led his country to great effect since assuming the captaincy in the wake of South Africa's disastrous showing at the 2003 50-over World Cup and continues to lead from the front in all forms of the game. The combative opener endured a difficult time with the bat at the 2007 World Twenty20 – amassing a disappointing 94 runs in five innings – but showed his liking for the 20-over format of the game with some stellar performances in the 2007 Indian Premier League. His competition total of 441 runs at 49.00 did much to propel the Rajasthan Royals along the road to winning the inaugural title.

SUPPORTING CAST

AB de Villiers: A calming influence with the bat and an electric presence in the field, the Pretoria batsman has become an integral part of the South African line-up.

Herschelle Gibbs: South Africa's most explosive batsman in limited-overs cricket. He is one of only four players in the history of the game to hit six sixes in an over.

Albie Morkel: A hard-hitting left-handed batsman and an effective fast-medium bowler, Albie Morkel, the older brother of Morne, was born to play 20-over cricket.

Morne Morkel: Has emerged as one of the most exciting fast-bowling prospects in world cricket. His metronomic line outside off stump makes him ideal for T20 cricket.

Dale Steyn: The most talked-about fast bowler on the planet, it is time for the spearhead of the South African attack to make an impact at a major global tournament.

The Qualifiers

Hundreds of international matches may have been played around the world during the 2008 season, but you can guarantee the tension would have been at its highest in Belfast from 2 to 5 August when six teams fought it out for three 2009 ICC World Twenty20 qualifying spots. Those who made it through the high-octane competition now have a chance to perform on the global stage.

Ireland (Group A)

Ever since they secured a spot in the 2007 World Cup, via a second-place finish in the 2005 ICC Continental Cup, Ireland have enjoyed their best times on a cricket field. When many thought that simply being in the Caribbean among the world's greatest players would be cause enough for celebration among the Irish players, they added to their supporters' already numerous smiles by first tying with Bangladesh and then, on St Patrick's Day, beating Pakistan by three wickets to qualify for the second phase. The Super Eights were a step too far and, although they lost their first four games, they did pick up an impressive, eyebrow-raising consolation victory over Bangladesh.

Wins over world cricket's main players have been hard to come by for Ireland since then, although they continue to enjoy success in the game's second tier. They won the ICC Intercontinental Cup in 2007 and collected a third European title in 2008. But in January 2007, they came up short in the World Cricket League in Kenya – the qualification tournament for the 2007 ICC World Twenty20 – losing four of their five games. They made amends in Belfast 18 months later though, beating Scotland and Kenya en route to qualification for the 2009 ICC World Twenty20. Don't bet against them producing another shock.

Star player: Niall O'Brien
A combative wicketkeeper-batsman who made has gained T20 experience with Kent and Northamptonshire, Niall O'Brien scored a measured 72 as Ireland pulled off the shock of the tournament by beating Pakistan. If Ireland are to pull off a shock on this occasion, they will need O'Brien to score heavily.

Netherlands (Group B)

The Netherlands have enjoyed the odd moment of success on the international cricket stage. They recorded a morale-boosting win over Namibia at the

Niall O'Brien: The wicketkeeper-batsman has used the experience gained in the Twenty20 Cup for Northamptonshire Steelbacks to help Ireland's cause.

92 The Qualifiers

Ryan ten Doeschate: The Essex Eagles all-rounder has shone for the Netherlands in recent times.

2003 World Cup in South Africa and then went on to beat Scotland in the 2007 edition of the tournament in the Caribbean. Not bad for a country with only 6,000 registered cricketers.

They finished an agonizing one place away from securing a spot at the inaugural ICC World Twenty20 in South Africa in 2007, losing out to Kenya and Scotland (by the slender margin of two runs), and travelled to Belfast in August 2008 for the 2009 ICC World Twenty20 qualification tournament determined not to make the same mistake. Although they suffered a surprise defeat to Canada, their opening 19-run win against Kenya was more than enough to see them through to the second phase. Between the Dutch and an automatic qualifying berth were Scotland. Ryan ten Doeschate (3 for 23) shone with the ball as Scotland slipped from 50 for 0 in the tenth over to 107 for 8; the Netherlands made short work of the target and won with an over to spare.

This will be a fourth appearance at a major global cricket tournament for the Dutch, but drawn alongside Pakistan and England, it is difficult to see them adding to their tally of wins.

Star player: Ryan ten Doeschate
Now an integral part of the Essex line-up in all forms of the game, South Africa-born Ryan ten Doeschate made the most of his Dutch ancestry to forge a career in international cricket. And how pleased the Netherlands must be to have him: the 28-year-old all-rounder has been their star performer with both bat and ball.

Scotland (Group D)
In recent times Scotland have started to become regular participants at major international tournaments, but although they have qualified for two 50-over World Cups (in 1999 and 2007) and for the inaugural ICC World Twenty20 (also in 2007) they have still to record their first victory on the game's biggest stage.

The Scots put up a brave showing in South Africa in the only match against Pakistan – their other game, against India, was lost to rain. The scoreboard may have recorded a comfortable 51-run win for Pakistan, but take Shahid Afridi (a murderous seven-ball 22 and 4 for 19) out of the equation and there was little to separate the two sides. The Scots left the tournament with their heads held high.

They travelled to Belfast in August 2008 keen on securing a spot for the 2009 ICC World Twenty20 and made heavy weather of it. After losing to Ireland in their opening game, they beat Bermuda by eight wickets to keep their tournament hopes alive and then collapsed to a five-wicket defeat in the semi-final. It left Scotland with their biggest game of the season: a must-win encounter against Kenya for the final qualification spot. Scotland held their nerve when it mattered and cantered to a nine-wicket victory. The third spot – made available by Zimbabwe's withdrawal from the competition – was theirs.

Star player: Ryan Watson
A hard-hitting batsman, an effective medium-pace bowler and captain, Ryan Watson is crucial to Scotland's hopes. He has made some major contributions to Scotland's cause, including an impressive 80 against Pakistan in 2006 on his ODI debut. A repeat performance in a T20 match could see Scotland past the winning post for the first time in an international tournament.

Twenty20 World Cup 2009: Tournament Fill-in Chart

Group Stage

Group	Date	Team	Score	v	Team	Score	Venue	Result
B	5 June	Netherlands	163-6	v	England	162-5	Lord's	Neths win by 4 wickets
D	6 June	Scotland	89-4	v	New Zealand	90-3	The Oval (7 overs)	NZ win by 7 wickets
C	6 June	Australia	169-7	v	West Indies	172-3	The Oval	WI win by 7 wickets
A	6 June	Bangladesh	155-8	v	India	180-5	Trent Bridge	India win by 25 runs
D	7 June	Scotland	81	v	South Africa	211-5	The Oval	SA win by 130 runs
B	7 June	England	185-5	v	Pakistan	137-7	The Oval	Eng win by 48 runs
A	8 June	Bangladesh	137-8	v	Ireland	138-4	Trent Bridge	Ireland win by 6 wickets
C	8 June	Australia	159-9	v	Sri Lanka	160-4	Trent Bridge	Sri Lanka win by 6 wickets
B	9 June	Pakistan	175-5	v	Netherlands	93	Lord's	Pakistan win by 82 runs
D	9 June	New Zealand	127-5	v	South Africa	128-7	Lord's	SA win by 1 run
A	10 June	India	113-2	v	Ireland	112-8	Trent Bridge (8 overs)	India win by 8 wickets
C	10 June	Sri Lanka	192-5	v	West Indies	177-5	Trent Bridge	Sri Lanka win by 15 runs

Final Group Tables

Top two teams from each group qualify for the Super Eights

GROUP A: India, Bangladesh, Ireland

Seed	Team	P	W	L	NR	T	Pts	NRR
1	1. India	2	2	0	0	0	4	1.23
	2. Ireland	2	1	1	0	0	2	-0.16
2	3. Bangladesh	2	0	2	0	0	0	-0.99

Winner qualifies for Group E, runner-up qualifies for Group F

GROUP B: Pakistan, England, Netherlands

Team	P	W	L	NR	T	Pts	NRR	Seed
1. England	2	1	1	0	0	2	+1.18	2
2. Pakistan	2	1	1	0	0	2	+0.85	1
3. Netherlands	2	1	1	0	0	2	-2.03	

Winner qualifies for Group F, runner-up qualifies for Group E

GROUP C: Australia, Sri Lanka, West Indies

Seed	Team	P	W	L	NR	T	Pts	NRR
2	1. Sri Lanka	2	2	0	0	0	4	0.63
	2. W. Indies	2	1	1	0	0	2	0.71
1	3. Australia	2	0	2	0	0	0	-1.33

Winner qualifies for Group E, runner-up qualifies for Group F

GROUP D: New Zealand, South Africa, Scotland

Team	P	W	L	NR	T	Pts	NRR	Seed
1. S. Africa	2	2	0	0	0	4	3.28	2
2. N. Zealand	2	1	1	0	0	2	0.31	1
3. Scotland	2	0	2	0	0	0	-5.21	

Winner qualifies for Group F, runner-up qualifies for Group E

Super Eights

Group	Date	Team	Score		Team	Score	Venue	Result
F	11 June	A2 Ireland	115	v	D1 N Zealand	198-5	Trent Bridge	NZ win by 83 runs
E	11 June	B2 England	111	v	D2 S Africa	114-3	Trent Bridge	SA win by 7 wickets
F	12 June	B1 Pakistan	131-9	v	C2 Sri Lanka	150-7	Lord's	SL win by 19 runs
E	12 June	A1 India	153-7	v	C1 W. Indies	156-3	Lord's	WI win by 7 wickets
E	13 June	C1 W. Indies	163-9	v	D2 S Africa	183-7	The Oval	SA win by 20 runs
F	13 June	D1 N. Zealand	99	v	B1 Pakistan	100-4	The Oval	Pak win by 6 wickets
F	14 June	A2 Ireland	135-7	v	C2 Sri Lanka	144-9	Lord's	SL win by 9 runs
E	14 June	A1 India	150-5	v	B2 England	153-7	Lord's	Eng win by 3 runs
E	15 June	B2 England	161-6	v	C1 W. Indies	82-5	The Oval	WI win by 5 wickets (D/L)
F	15 June	B1 Pakistan	159-5	v	A2 Ireland	120-9	The Oval	Pak win by 39 runs
F	16 June	D1 N. Zealand	110	v	C2 Sri Lanka	158-5	Trent Bridge	SL win by 48 runs
E	16 June	D2 S Africa	130-5	v	A1 India	118-8	Trent Bridge	SA win by 12 runs

Final Super Eight Tables

Group E: Winners Groups A and C, Runners-up B and D

Team	P	W	L	NR	T	Pts	NRR
1. South Africa	3	3	0	0	0	6	0.58
2. W. Indies	3	2	1	0	0	4	0.06
3. England	3	1	2	0	0	2	-0.4
4. India	3	0	3	0	0	0	-0.30

Winner qualifies for semi-final 1; runner-up qualifies for semi-final 2

Group F: Winners Groups B and D, Runners-up A and C

Team	P	W	L	NR	T	Pts	NRR
1. Sri Lanka	3	3	0	0	0	6	1.27
2. Pakistan	3	2	1	0	0	4	1.19
3. New Zealand	3	1	2	0	0	2	-0.17
4. Ireland	3	0	3	0	0	0	-2.18

Winner qualifies for semi-final 2; runner-up qualifies for semi-final 1

Semi-finals

Date	Team	Score		Team	Score	Venue	Result
18 June	E1 South Africa	142-5	v	F2 Pakistan	149-4	Trent Bridge	Pakistan win by 7 runs
19 June	F1 Sri Lanka	158-5	v	E2 West Indies	101	Trent Bridge	Sri Lanka win by 57 runs

Final

Date	Team	Score		Team	Score	Venue	Result
21 June	TBC Pakistan	139-2	v	TBC Sri Lanka	138-6	Lord's	Pakistan win by 8 wickets

Women's Twenty20 World Cup 2009

Women's cricket has always suffered from an image problem. For too long, coverage of the game has been limited to a few millimetres of column space, at best, in the world's newspapers. But women's cricket has improved immeasurably in recent years, and in 2009 the players have been given the opportunity to showcase their considerable talents alongside the men.

It is another example of the revolutionary nature of Twenty20 cricket. The three-hour duration of matches means that more than one match can be played at the same venue on the same day and for that reason – although cynics might suggest it is just another project cooked up by marketing men to raise a bit of extra cash – the inaugural ICC Women's World Twenty20 will be staged at the same time as the men's. There will be eight teams, with all of the group games to be played at Taunton, but the semi-finals will be staged prior to the equivalent men's ties – at Trent Bridge and The Oval – and the final will be played at Lord's. The fact that they have been trusted to play a showcase game at the world's most prestigious ground is seen as a huge compliment to the women's game.

THE TEAMS

Group A
Australia
The current No.1-ranked team in women's cricket, Australia will enter the tournament as favourites. An excellent combination of youth and experience, they are expected to be led by hard-hitting batter Karen Rolton. Also watch out for Lisa Sthalekar, widely regarded as one of the leading all-rounders in the women's game.
Star Player: Karen Rolton

New Zealand
New Zealand will be looking to bounce back from disappointing recent defeats to both England and Australia. The team will be led by Haidee Tiffen, and the performances of all-rounders Aimee Mason and Nicola Brown will be crucial to their success. However, they can look to the fact that the last time they were in England – in the summer of 2007 – they enjoyed a series win. Anything short of a place in the semi-finals will come as a huge disappointment.
Star Player: Haidee Tiffen

South Africa
Times are tough for women's cricket in South Africa. Their performances on home soil at the 2005 World Cup were so disappointing that they were forced to qualify for the 2009 event. They have also had to suffer the defection of their best player, Johmari Logtenberg, to golf. With Cri-Zelda Brits leading them, progress beyond the group stages would signify a huge improvement for the South Africans.
Star Player: Cri-Zelda Brits

West Indies
Perhaps the unknown quantity of the Women's World Twenty20 given that, apart from a few matches against Ireland and the Netherlands, they have played little cricket since the 2005 World Cup – where they just missed out on the semi-finals. Come June, their lack of time in the middle may well count against them.
Star Player: Stacy-Ann Camille-Ann King

Group B
England
The hosts have every reason to enter the competition full of confidence following some brilliant displays against Australia and New Zealand in early 2008. In Charlotte Edwards they have the current ICC Women's Cricketer of the Year. Others to

Haidee Tiffen: Nothing short of a place in the semi-finals should suffice for the New Zealand captain.

watch out for are Claire Taylor and highly promising wicketkeeper Sarah Taylor.
Star Player: Charlotte Edwards

India
One of the big four of the women's game – alongside Australia, England and New Zealand – India will start among the pre-tournament favourites following their comfortable success in the Asia Cup in May 2008. Led by Mithali Raj; expect fireworks from Jhulan Goswami, the ICC Player of the Year in 2007 and one of the most feared bowlers in the women's game.
Star Player: Jhulan Goswami

Pakistan
Qualifiers for the ICC Women's World Twenty20; the women's game in Pakistan is still very much in its formative years. They suffered a disappointing campaign in the 2008 Asia Cup – registering just one victory, against Bangladesh. Asmavia Iqbal has huge talent with the ball and Bismah Maroof has the ability to score runs at the highest level with the bat, but the tournament for Pakistan will be all about gaining valuable experience.
Star Player: Asmavia Iqbal

Sri Lanka
Sri Lanka made it to the final of the Asia Cup in 2008, only to find themselves on the wrong end of an eight-wicket walloping by India. And they will have to overcome the same opponents – as well as hosts England – if they want to progress to the knockout stages. They will rely heavily on the performances of captain Shashikala Siriwardene, an influential and effective player with both bat and ball.
Star Player: Shashikala Siriwardene

Fixtures
Group Matches (all played at Taunton)

Thursday, 11 June 2009
Group A: West Indies v South Africa
Group B: India v England

Friday, 12 June 2009
Group A: Australia v New Zealand
Group B: Pakistan v Sri Lanka

Saturday, 13 June 2009
Group A: West Indies v New Zealand
Group B: India v Pakistan

Sunday, 14 June 2009
Group A: Australia v West Indies
Group B: England v Sri Lanka

Monday, 15 June 2009
Group A: New Zealand v South Africa
Group B: India v Sri Lanka

Tuesday, 16 June 2009
Group A: Australia v South Africa
Group B: England v Pakistan

Semi-finals
Thursday, 18 June 2009 (at Trent Bridge)
Runner-up Group B v Winner Group A
Friday, 19 June 2009 (at The Oval)
Winner Group A v Runner-up Group B

Final
Sunday, 21 June 2009
Winner SF A v Winner SF B
(at Lord's)

Jhulan Goswami: The Indian strike bowler is the most feared fast bowler in the women's game.

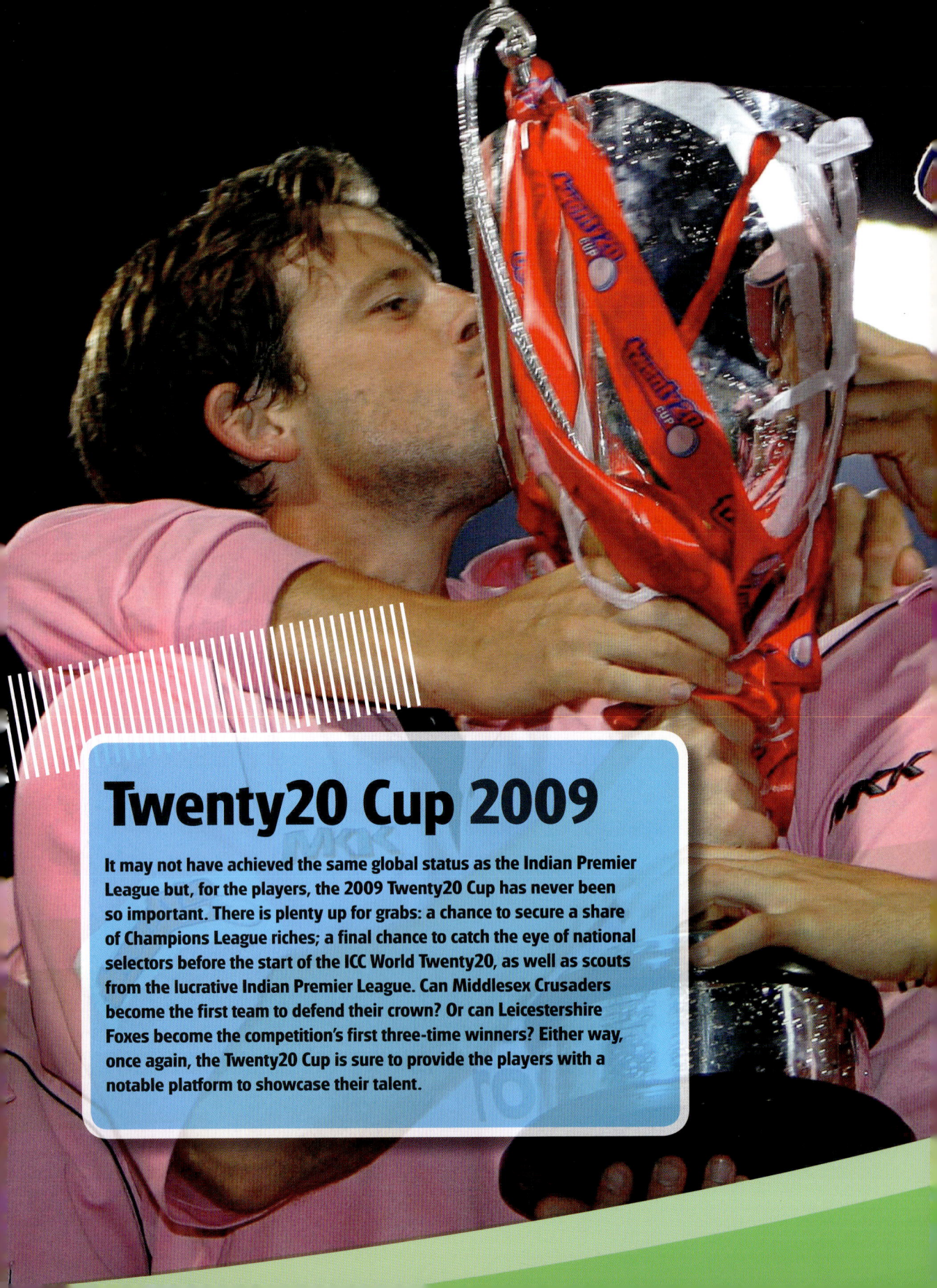

Twenty20 Cup 2009

It may not have achieved the same global status as the Indian Premier League but, for the players, the 2009 Twenty20 Cup has never been so important. There is plenty up for grabs: a chance to secure a share of Champions League riches; a final chance to catch the eye of national selectors before the start of the ICC World Twenty20, as well as scouts from the lucrative Indian Premier League. Can Middlesex Crusaders become the first team to defend their crown? Or can Leicestershire Foxes become the competition's first three-time winners? Either way, once again, the Twenty20 Cup is sure to provide the players with a notable platform to showcase their talent.

Enduring images from 2008:
Left: **Middlesex Crusaders:** Can the champions from 2008 repeat in 2009?
Top: **Marcus Trescothick:** He will try to show England fans how much he is missed.
Above: **Graham Napier:** Will be looking to enhance his reputation as an expert at T20.

The Counties

Derbyshire Scorpions (North Division)
Coach: John Morris
Ground: County Ground, Derby
(capacity: 9,500)
T20 Cup 2008 performance:
Group stage (P10, W3, L7)
T20 Cup best: Quarter-finals (2005)
Star Performer in 2008: Charl Langeveldt

A quarter-final appearance in 2005 apart, the Twenty20 Cup has proved a fruitless hunting ground for Derbyshire and 2008, under a new captain, Rikki Clarke, proved no exception. A thumping 47-run win over Yorkshire – with Kolpak signings Greg Smith (100) and Charl Langeveldt (4 for 9) the pick of the crop – promised great things off the back of their opening five-wicket defeat to Durham, but it proved a false dawn. If 200 runs is the batting benchmark for a good tournament, then only two of Derbyshire's batsmen passed muster – Smith (275 runs) and Wavell Hinds (283). And it was runs, or the lack of them, that lay at the root of their 2008 Twenty20 Cup woes; that Lancashire cruised past their season-high total (153 for 5) with 3.4 overs to spare only highlighted the deficiencies in the batting department. Heavily reliant on the form of their Kolpak signings, it's difficult to see the Twenty20 gloom lifting in 2009.

Batting: Leading Averages in 2008 (qualification: 100 runs)

Player	M	I	NO	R	HS	Ave	SR	50	100
WW Hinds	10	10	2	283	72*	35.37	103.39	2	0
GM Smith	10	10	1	275	100*	30.55	127.31	1	1
DJ Pipe	10	9	1	162	45	20.25	129.60	0	0
FD Telo	8	8	0	134	66	16.75	107.20	0	0
DJ Birch	10	9	2	108	25	15.42	87.80	0	0
R Clarke	9	9	1	121	36	15.12	104.31	0	0

Bowling: Leading Economy Rates in 2008 (qualification: 4 wickets)

Player	M	I	O	M	R	W	BBI	Ave	Econ	4w	5w
CK Langeveldt	7	7	21.0	1	118	8	4/9	14.75	5.61	1	0
ND Doshi	10	10	33.4	0	198	8	3/1	24.75	5.88	0	0
WW Hinds	10	8	18.0	0	124	4	2/14	31.00	6.88	0	0
GG Wagg	10	10	32.0	0	254	8	3/23	31.75	7.93	0	0
R Clarke	9	9	22.3	0	182	6	2/32	30.33	8.08	0	0
J Needham	10	9	21.0	0	172	4	1/4	43.00	8.19	0	0

Durham Dynamos (North Division)
Coach: Geoff Cook
Ground: Riverside Ground, Chester-le-Street
(capacity: 15,000)
T20 Cup 2008 performance:
Semi-finals (P12, W7, L2, T1, NR2)
T20 Cup best: Semi-finals (2008)
Star Performer in 2008: Phil Mustard

Durham are on the up. In 2007 they collected the first domestic trophy in their history and they entered 2008 determined to continue their trophy-winning ways. Paul Collingwood (5 for 14) set the tone in their opening five-wicket win over Derbyshire. South Africans Albie Morkel (4 for 30) and Dale Benkenstein (48) followed suit in a six-wicket win over Leicestershire and, although they suffered a 23-run reverse against Nottinghamshire, it was the last time they would taste defeat in the group stages. The rumpus over Durham's abandoned quarter-final clash against their White Rose neighbours could have done much to stop a lesser side's momentum, but not Durham: they beat Glamorgan in a rearranged tie by 44 runs. The county's first taste of Twenty20 finals day turned out to be a bitter one – thanks to a rampant display from Middlesex's Tyron Henderson – but Durham have become strong challengers on all fronts.

Batting: Leading Averages in 2008 (qualification: 100 runs)

Player	M	I	NO	R	HS	Ave	SR	50	100
DM Benkenstein	11	10	4	239	48*	39.83	123.83	0	0
JA Morkel	9	8	3	150	54*	30.00	154.63	1	0
P Mustard	11	11	0	303	61	27.54	135.26	1	0
WR Smith	11	11	1	245	51	24.50	122.50	1	0
MJ Di Venuto	10	10	0	115	40	11.50	115.00	0	0

Bowling: Leading Economy Rates in 2008 (qualification: 4 wickets)

Player	M	I	O	M	R	W	BBI	Ave	Econ	4w	5w
SM Pollock	11	11	38.4	1	210	13	2/15	16.15	5.43	0	0
PD Collingwood	3	2	8.0	0	46	7	5/14	6.57	5.75	0	1
LE Plunkett	11	11	36.4	0	228	13	3/16	17.53	6.21	0	0
GR Breese	11	9	26.0	0	166	8	3/17	20.75	6.38	0	0
SJ Harmison	7	6	20.4	0	144	9	4/38	16.00	6.96	1	0
JA Morkel	9	5	19.0	0	154	6	4/30	25.66	8.10	1	0

The Counties (Derbyshire – Glamorgan)

Derbyshire – Glamorgan

Essex Eagles (South Division)
Coach: Paul Grayson
Ground: County Cricket Ground, Chelmsford (capacity: 6,500)
T20 Cup 2008 performance:
Semi-finals (P14, W7, L4, T1)
T20 Cup best: Semi-finals (2006, 2008)
Star Performer in 2008: Graham Napier

Essex, led by Graham Napier's heroics, enjoyed a headline-grabbing 2008 Twenty20 Cup campaign before running into an in-form Kent in the semi-finals. A solitary victory in their opening three games was hardly the form of potential winners, but three successive wins put their trophy-winning aspirations back on track. A loss against Kent could have stalled their momentum, but then came Napier's blitzkrieg against Sussex, and the confidence taken from that record-breaking 128-run victory carried them through to the quarter-finals. They brushed aside Northamptonshire, but then came Kent. It was a disappointing end to what had been a promising campaign. Napier (the sixth leading run-scorer and eighth leading wicket-taker) wasn't the only standout performer: Danish Kaneria was one of only five bowlers to pass the 20-wicket mark; and four of their batsmen (Napier, James Foster, Mark Pettini and Grant Flower) passed 200 runs. If the players can repeat that form in 2009, they will be strong contenders for the trophy.

Batting: Leading Averages in 2008 (qualification: 100 runs)

Player	M	I	NO	R	HS	Ave	SR	50	100
JS Foster	12	11	3	295	50*	36.87	140.47	1	0
GR Napier	12	11	1	326	152*	32.60	195.20	0	1
ML Pettini	9	9	0	234	66	26.00	129.28	2	0
GW Flower	12	11	2	203	39*	22.55	106.84	0	0
JER Gallian	8	8	0	163	55	20.37	101.24	1	0
RN ten Doeschate	12	10	1	138	35	15.33	160.46	0	0

Bowling: Leading Economy Rates in 2008 (qualification: 4 wickets)

Player	M	I	O	M	R	W	BBI	Ave	Econ	4w	5w
Danish Kaneria	12	12	45.1	0	276	20	4/22	13.80	6.11	1	0
DD Masters	12	12	39.0	3	256	10	2/17	25.60	6.56	0	0
RS Bopara	3	2	8.0	0	54	4	3/36	13.50	6.75	0	0
RN ten Doeschate	12	10	35.5	0	243	13	4/24	18.69	6.78	1	0
GR Napier	12	12	40.1	2	282	16	4/10	17.62	7.02	1	0
MA Chambers	11	11	27.0	0	221	10	3/31	22.10	8.18	0	0
JD Middlebrook	12	10	20.0	0	180	4	3/13	45.00	9.00	0	0

Glamorgan Dragons (Mid/Wales/West Division)
Coach: Adrian Shaw
Ground: Sophia Gardens, Cardiff (capacity: 16,000)
T20 Cup 2008 performance:
Quarter-finals (P9, W3, L3, NR3)
T20 Cup best: Semi-finals (2004)
Star Performer in 2008: Robert Croft

Two washouts in the first three games set the tone for Glamorgan's 2008 Twenty20 Cup campaign. By the time they faced off against Worcestershire in the final group game, they had lost three matches to the weather, suffered three defeats and recorded a mere two victories. They may not have known it at the time, but a six-wicket win over Worcestershire threw them a lifeline. As it was, they left New Road hoping for better fortune next time round. Lady Luck did not wait that long. On 14 July 2008, Glamorgan became the main beneficiaries of Yorkshire's oversight in playing an ineligible player: the stream of single points gained from the no-results had left them the best of the rest – and they took the White Rose county's place in the quarter-final line-up. The respite, however, was brief. Chasing 164 for victory over Durham, they slumped to 119 all out. The storm clouds gathered around Cardiff once again. Glamorgan's supporters will be hoping they lift in 2009.

Batting: Leading Averages in 2008 (qualification: 100 runs)

Player	M	I	NO	R	HS	Ave	SR	50	100
HH Gibbs	8	6	1	281	98	56.20	143.36	2	0
JWM Dalrymple	9	7	2	152	38*	30.40	118.75	0	0
MA Wallace	9	7	3	115	28*	28.75	191.66	0	0
RBD Croft	9	6	0	145	50	24.16	134.25	1	0
DL Hemp	9	8	1	146	38*	20.85	110.60	0	0
MJ Powell	9	7	0	134	36	19.14	109.83	0	0

Bowling: Leading Economy Rates in 2008 (qualification: 4 wickets)

Player	M	I	O	M	R	W	BBI	Ave	Econ	4w	5w
RBD Croft	9	8	31.4	0	213	9	3/12	23.66	6.72	0	0
JWM Dalrymple	9	7	15.0	0	109	7	2/22	15.57	7.26	0	0
DA Cosker	9	8	31.0	0	233	10	3/32	23.30	7.51	0	0
DS Harrison	9	8	26.0	0	198	6	2/30	33.00	7.61	0	0
RE Watkins	8	7	23.0	0	195	11	2/20	17.72	8.47	0	0
JAR Harris	4	3	10.0	0	89	4	3/41	22.25	8.90	0	0
AG Wharf	6	6	18.0	0	214	5	2/46	42.80	11.88	0	0

The Counties

Gloucestershire Gladiators (Mid/Wales/West Division)
Coach: John Bracewell
Ground: County Cricket Ground, Nevil Road, Bristol (capacity: 8,000)
T20 Cup 2008 performance:
Group stage (P10, W1, L5, T1, NR3)
T20 Cup best: Runners-up (2007)
Star Performer in 2008: Hamish Marshall

Gloucestershire were the undisputed kings of one-day cricket in the late 1990s and early 2000s, a period that saw them collect eight trophies in six years, but the Twenty20 Cup has never been kind to them. They reached the semi-finals in 2003, the last eight in 2006, and suffered final heartbreak a year later, but if the West Country men were looking to 2008 as the year they were going to break their tournament duck, they would have been bitterly disappointed. The weather played its part, but a solitary victory in the seven matches they played tells its own story. Of the batsmen, only New Zealander Hamish Marshall topped the 200-run mark; and the bowlers fared little better (Mark Hardinges was the leading wicket-taker with seven). Gloucestershire finished bottom of the Mid/Wales/West Division with a paltry six points. Things can only get better in 2009, but those trophy-laden days are starting to feel like a distant memory.

Batting: Leading Averages in 2008 (qualification: 100 runs)

Player	M	I	NO	R	HS	Ave	SR	50	100
MJ North	7	7	2	194	45	38.80	116.86	0	0
HJH Marshall	7	7	0	203	59	29.00	137.16	1	0
CG Taylor	7	7	1	169	66	28.16	129.00	1	0

Bowling: Leading Economy Rates in 2008 (qualification: 4 wickets)

Player	M	I	O	M	R	W	BBI	Ave	Econ	4w	5w
AJ Harris	3	3	12.0	1	78	5	2/19	15.60	6.50	0	0
MA Hardinges	7	7	24.0	0	170	7	4/30	24.28	7.08	1	0
ID Fisher	7	7	23.0	0	168	5	3/20	33.60	7.30	0	0
SP Kirby	5	5	19.0	1	145	4	1/20	36.25	7.63	0	0
WD Rudge	5	5	14.2	0	116	4	2/26	29.00	8.09	0	0
J Lewis	4	4	14.0	0	131	4	3/22	32.75	9.35	0	0

Hampshire Hawks (South Division)
Coach: Paul Terry
Ground: Rose Bowl, Southampton (capacity: 22,000)
T20 Cup 2008 performance:
Group stage (P14, W4, L10, D0)
T20 Cup best: Quarter-finals (2004)
Star Performer in 2008: Michael Carberry

With finals day due to be staged at their very own Rose Bowl stadium, Hampshire had every motivation, entering the 2008 season, to improve their disappointing Twenty20 Cup record – they had made just one quarter-final appearance (in 2004). A record of five wins and three losses in their first eight games – with Michael Carberry, in particular, impressing with the bat – left them in joint second place in the group with two games to go, a home-and-away double-header against Essex. Carberry hit 51 off 42 balls at the top of the order to propel Hampshire to 164 for 6, before Essex scrambled 11 off the final over to force a tie. The result left the reverse fixture at Chelmsford as a straight knockout match for a place in the semi-finals. Home advantage won out: Essex cantered to a 54-run victory and Hampshire were left to rue another lost opportunity. If they can make it out of the tough South Division group stage – the group provided three of the four semi-finalists in 2008 – they have a squad of players capable of challenging for Twenty20 Cup honours in 2009.

Batting: Leading Averages in 2008 (qualification: 100 runs)

Player	M	I	NO	R	HS	Ave	SR	50	100
MA Carberry	10	10	1	334	58	37.11	124.62	4	0
MJ Lumb	10	10	0	315	63	31.50	150.71	2	0
MJ Brown	6	6	1	130	44	26.00	121.49	0	0
IJ Harvey	9	9	0	197	34	21.88	128.75	0	0
SM Ervine	9	9	1	173	46	21.62	153.09	0	0

Bowling: Leading Economy Rates in 2008 (qualification: 4 wickets)

Player	M	I	O	M	R	W	BBI	Ave	Econ	4w	5w
CT Tremlett	4	4	15.4	0	106	7	4/25	15.14	6.76	1	0
IJ Harvey	9	7	26.0	0	189	7	2/20	27.00	7.26	0	0
AD Mascarenhas	4	4	16.0	0	118	8	3/12	14.75	7.37	0	0
BV Taylor	9	9	33.0	1	256	6	2/18	42.66	7.75	0	0
GA Lamb	10	10	33.3	0	265	8	2/25	33.12	7.91	0	0
M Hayward	10	10	35.0	1	278	13	3/22	21.38	7.94	0	0

The Counties: Gloucestershire – Lancashire

Gloucestershire – Lancashire

Kent Spitfires (South Division)
Coach: Graham Ford
Ground: St Lawrence Ground, Canterbury (capacity: 15,000)
T20 Cup 2008 performance: Runners-up (P13, W8, L5)
T20 Cup best: Champions (2007)
Star Performer in 2008: Joe Denly

Yasir Arafat (4 for 17) ensured defending champions Kent got the 2008 Twenty20 Cup campaign off to a rollicking start with a six-wicket victory over Sussex. Their good form continued: after seven games, their record of won five lost two was as good as anyone's in the country. Two successive six-run defeats, however, put their chance of becoming the first side to defend the trophy in jeopardy, before Yasir Arafat ended the group stage as he had begun it: with a match-winning bowling performance (3 for 12) against Sussex. Kent's reward was a tough away trip to face Warwickshire in the last eight: they eased to an impressive 42-run victory. They overcame Essex in the semi-finals and played a full part in an exhilarating final – only to go down to Middlesex by three runs. Cruelly denied a place in the Champions League, Kent will be out to prove a point in 2009. They have a squad more than capable of making one.

Batting: Leading Averages in 2008 (qualification: 100 runs)

Player	M	I	NO	R	HS	Ave	SR	50	100
Azhar Mahmood	13	13	6	294	55	42.00	168.00	1	0
JL Denly	13	13	0	451	91	34.69	118.99	5	0
DI Stevens	13	13	5	267	69	33.37	146.70	1	0
RWT Key	13	13	0	345	52	26.53	133.72	1	0
Yasir Arafat	13	8	2	130	42	21.66	154.76	0	0
JM Kemp	11	11	0	201	49	18.27	121.73	0	0
M van Jaarsveld	12	11	0	140	32	12.72	121.73	0	0

Bowling: Leading Economy Rates in 2008 (qualification: 4 wickets)

Player	M	I	O	M	R	W	BBI	Ave	Econ	4w	5w
JC Tredwell	13	12	41.0	1	264	16	3/9	16.50	6.43	0	0
R McLaren	13	13	43.5	0	334	15	3/28	22.26	7.61	0	0
Azhar Mahmood	13	13	47.5	0	368	15	3/27	24.53	7.69	0	0
Yasir Arafat	13	13	44.0	0	341	23	4/47	14.82	7.75	2	0
SJ Cook	12	12	46.0	0	379	11	3/21	34.45	8.23	0	0
DI Stevens	13	8	16.0	0	140	5	2/29	28.00	8.75	0	0

Lancashire Lightning (North Division)
Coach: Mike Watkinson
Ground: Old Trafford, Manchester (capacity: 19,000)
T20 Cup 2008 performance: Quarter-finals (P14, W4, L10, D0)
T20 Cup best: Runners-up (2005)
Star Performer in 2008: Mal Loye

Serial contenders for the Twenty20 Cup – they were semi-finalists in 2004 and 2007 and runners-up in 2005 – Lancashire saw 2008 as the year they would finally break their tournament duck. Three successive – and comprehensive – victories in their first three games was a serious statement of intent; before three consecutive defeats – two of them, painfully, against Yorkshire – almost derailed their campaign. They rallied well to record home-and-away victories over Nottinghamshire and a crushing nine-wicket win over Derbyshire (in which Lou Vincent scored an unbeaten 102), to take their place in the quarter-finals. But that was where any dreams of victory came to an end. They ran into the competition's form side, Middlesex, and lost by 12 runs. It is nine years since Lancashire last picked up one of county cricket's major prizes (they won the 40-over National League in 1999), and the Red Rose county are fast acquiring the tag of nearly men. It is a situation they will be desperate to reverse in 2009.

Batting: Leading Averages in 2008 (qualification: 100 runs)

Player	M	I	NO	R	HS	Ave	SR	50	100
MB Loye	10	10	2	275	54*	34.37	118.53	2	0
L Vincent	10	10	2	268	102*	33.50	127.01	2	1
F du Plessis	11	8	1	202	57*	28.85	114.12	1	0
SG Law	11	10	1	192	54	21.33	123.07	1	0
SJ Croft	11	8	1	134	29	19.14	102.29	0	0
KW Hogg	11	8	1	120	44	17.14	148.14	0	0

Bowling: Leading Economy Rates in 2008 (qualification: 4 wickets)

Player	M	I	O	M	R	W	BBI	Ave	Econ	4w	5w
A Flintoff	6	3	10.0	0	56	8	4/12	7.00	5.60	1	0
G Chapple	5	5	16.0	0	95	5	2/23	19.00	5.93	0	0
SI Mahmood	9	9	31.0	0	193	12	3/12	16.08	6.22	0	0
G Keedy	5	5	11.4	1	81	6	4/15	13.50	6.94	1	0
DG Cork	8	8	26.0	1	188	8	2/24	23.50	7.23	0	0
SJ Marshall	9	8	26.1	0	190	14	4/21	13.57	7.26	1	0
KW Hogg	11	10	29.0	0	219	6	2/31	36.50	7.55	0	0
F du Plessis	11	8	19.0	0	147	9	2/13	16.33	7.73	0	0
SJ Croft	11	11	25.2	0	209	6	3/6	34.83	8.25	0	0

The Counties

Leicestershire Foxes (North Division)
Coach: Tim Boon
Ground: Grace Road, Leicester (capacity: 12,000)
T20 Cup 2008 performance: Group stages (P10, W2, L7, NR1)
T20 Cup best: Winners (2004, 2006)
Star Performer in 2008: James Allenby

Expectations are understandably high at Grace Road when it comes to the Twenty20 Cup: Leicestershire are the only side in the tournament's history to have won the competition twice (in 2004 and 2006). However, they will be seeking to forget their performances in 2008 – they endured a miserable campaign. They may have lost several personnel over the course of the winter – including England paceman and Twenty20 specialist Stuart Broad (to Nottinghamshire) – but seven defeats in their first seven matches tells its own story. Even the two victories they picked up in their last three games did little to hide the gloom. Of the batsmen, only HD Ackerman passed the 200-run mark; James Allenby (who picked up a competition-leading two five-wicket hauls) stood out with the ball; but, when all is said and done, the 2009 campaign cannot come quickly enough for Leicestershire. They are a side with a Twenty20 reputation to salvage.

Batting: Leading Averages in 2008 (qualification: 100 runs)

Player	M	I	NO	R	HS	Ave	SR	50	100
HD Ackerman	8	8	2	239	63	39.83	112.73	3	0
J Allenby	9	9	1	190	57	23.75	109.82	2	0
HH Dippenaar	9	8	0	148	47	18.50	102.06	0	0
PA Nixon	9	9	0	163	42	18.11	96.44	0	0
J du Toit	9	9	0	117	25	13.00	110.37	0	0

Bowling: Leading Economy Rates in 2008 (qualification: 4 wickets)

Player	M	I	O	M	R	W	BBI	Ave	Econ	4w	5w
CW Henderson	9	9	33.3	0	205	8	2/15	25.62	6.11	0	0
MN Malik	9	9	32.0	1	216	11	4/16	19.63	6.75	1	0
J Allenby	9	7	21.3	0	148	14	5/21	10.57	6.88	0	2
D du Preez	5	5	19.0	0	157	6	2/31	26.16	8.26	0	0
GJP Kruger	6	6	19.0	0	172	4	1/26	43.00	9.05	0	0

Middlesex Crusaders (South Division)
Coach: Toby Radford
Ground: Lord's Cricket Ground, London (capacity: 30,000)
T20 Cup 2008 performance: Champions (P13, W11, L2)
T20 Cup best: Champions (2008)
Star Performer in 2008: Dawid Malan

Sixteen years had passed since Middlesex last collected a piece of silverware – the 1992 Sunday League title – and with a solitary quarter-final appearance in 2005 their best-ever showing in the competition, few thought the 2008 Twenty20 Cup would see the end of the long trophy drought. But Middlesex rocketed out of the starting blocks, winning their first five games to shoot to the top of the South Division table. Two successive defeats later, doubts may have started to creep in, but Middlesex dismissed them in style: they won their last three group games to top the table; edged past Lancashire in the quarter-finals; and then thumped Durham in the semi-finals. The final against Kent was a classic: Middlesex won the trophy by the slender margin of three runs and the right to become English cricket's first representatives in the Champions League. Dawid Malan, Owais Shah and Tyron Henderson shone with the bat; veteran Shaun Udal and his spin twin Murali Kartik starred with the ball. It's a tough act to follow in 2009.

Batting: Leading Averages in 2008 (qualification: 100 runs)

Player	M	I	NO	R	HS	Ave	SR	50	100
DJ Malan	12	10	5	306	103	61.20	139.09	1	1
OA Shah	4	4	1	136	75	45.33	158.13	1	0
T Henderson	12	11	4	281	64*	40.14	180.12	2	0
EJG Morgan	13	12	1	279	62	25.36	135.43	1	0
EC Joyce	13	12	3	227	47	25.22	107.07	0	0
BA Godleman	11	11	0	201	69	18.27	108.06	2	0

Bowling: Leading Economy Rates in 2008 (qualification: 4 wickets)

Player	M	I	O	M	R	W	BBI	Ave	Econ	4w	5w
SD Udal	13	13	48.0	0	299	12	3/19	24.91	6.22	0	0
M Kartik	11	11	42.0	0	282	14	2/15	20.14	6.71	0	0
ST Finn	5	5	16.0	0	115	8	3/22	14.37	7.18	0	0
T Henderson	12	12	47.0	0	349	21	4/29	16.61	7.42	1	0
DP Nannes	9	9	33.0	1	246	14	4/28	17.57	7.45	1	0
TJ Murtagh	13	13	50.0	0	400	20	3/15	20.00	8.00	0	0

Leicestershire – Nottinghamshire

Northamptonshire Steelbacks (Mid/Wales West Division)
Coach: David Capel
Ground: County Ground, Northampton (capacity: 6,500)
T20 Cup 2008 performance: Quarter-finals (P10, W6, L3, NR1)
T20 Cup best: Quarter-finals (2005, 2006, 2008)
Star Performer in 2008: Andrew Hall

A pair of quarter-final appearances apart (in 2005 and 2006), the Twenty20 Cup has never been a happy hunting ground for Northamptonshire and as the 2008 campaign kicked off, it would be fair to say they weren't high on anybody's list of potential winners. But former South Africa international Andrew Hall ensured they got off to a blistering start, hitting 54 in a win over Somerset and 66 – and a season-best 6 for 21 – in the victory over Worcestershire. Back-to-back victories over Gloucestershire kept the momentum going. Although successive defeats against Warwickshire and Glamorgan could have burst the bubble, a 24-run win in the reverse fixture against Glamorgan saw them continue their march to the quarter-finals. Not for the first time, however, that is where the journey came to an end. They lost to Essex by 59 runs. It was a disappointing end to what had been a promising campaign, but Northamptonshire have a talented squad and they could well be dark horses for success in 2009.

Batting: Leading Averages in 2008 (qualification: 100 runs)

Player	M	I	NO	R	HS	Ave	SR	50	100
AJ Hall	9	8	1	233	66*	33.28	114.77	3	0
RA White	11	11	2	288	94*	32.00	157.37	1	0
DJG Sales	11	10	2	253	71*	31.62	121.05	2	0
N Boje	11	6	2	115	58*	28.75	102.67	1	0
NJ O'Brien	11	11	1	217	69	21.70	157.24	1	0
L Klusener	11	8	2	116	41*	19.33	104.50	0	0
MH Wessels	11	10	2	143	43*	17.87	140.19	0	0

Bowling: Leading Economy Rates in 2008 (qualification: 4 wickets)

Player	M	I	O	M	R	W	BBI	Ave	Econ	4w	5w
JF Brown	9	9	30.0	0	203	7	2/31	29.00	6.76	0	0
N Boje	11	10	35.4	0	248	10	2/19	24.80	6.95	0	0
JJ van der Wath	10	10	36.0	1	255	7	1/14	36.42	7.08	0	0
AJ Hall	9	9	34.1	0	271	20	6/21	13.55	7.93	2	0
J Louw	11	11	39.0	0	325	17	3/18	19.11	8.33	0	0

Nottinghamshire Outlaws (North Division)
Coach: Mike Newell
Ground: Trent Bridge, Nottingham (capacity: 17,000)
T20 Cup 2008 performance: Group stages (P14, W4, L10, D0)
T20 Cup best: Runners-up (2006)
Star Performer in 2008: Samit Patel

Nottinghamshire had enjoyed the taste of the latter stages of the Twenty20 Cup in recent years – reaching the final in 2006 and the quarter-finals in 2007 – and clearly wanted more of it, starting their 2008 campaign in convincing fashion, with four victories – and one no-result – in their first five matches. But then their momentum came to a shuddering halt. Four straight defeats in their final four games saw them miss out on a quarter-final place by a solitary point. A lack of runs was Nottinghamshire's major problem – only Adam Voges (302) and Will Jefferson (209) passed the 200-run mark. The bowlers were more consistent, but the fact that not one of their leading bowlers had an economy rate of under six tells its own story, although the Notts attack was not helped by the absence of Ryan Sidebottom and Stuart Broad who were away on England duty. Expect better things of them in 2009.

Batting: Leading Averages in 2008 (qualification: 100 runs)

Player	M	I	NO	R	HS	Ave	SR	50	100
AC Voges	9	9	1	302	59	37.75	130.17	3	0
WI Jefferson	9	9	0	209	43	23.22	112.36	0	0
SR Patel	9	9	1	161	56	20.12	166.66	1	0
CMW Read	9	8	2	115	31	19.16	118.55	0	0
CL Cairns	9	9	1	153	50	19.12	128.57	1	0

Bowling: Leading Economy Rates in 2008 (qualification: 4 wickets)

Player	M	I	O	M	R	W	BBI	Ave	Econ	4w	5w
RS Ferley	7	7	26.0	0	163	9	3/17	18.11	6.26	0	0
SR Patel	9	9	29.0	0	187	10	3/22	18.70	6.44	0	0
DJ Pattinson	7	7	20.0	0	136	8	3/18	17.00	6.80	0	0
CE Shreck	5	5	15.0	2	103	6	4/22	17.16	6.86	1	0
AR Adams	9	9	33.0	0	257	9	2/23	28.55	7.78	0	0
MA Ealham	9	9	32.0	0	251	10	3/21	25.10	7.84	0	0

The Counties

Somerset Sabres (Mid/Wales/West Division)
Coach: Andrew Hurry
Ground: County Ground, Taunton (capacity: 6,500)
T20 Cup 2008 performance: Group stages (P10, W3, L4, NR3)
T20 Cup best: Champions (2005)
Star Performer in 2008: Marcus Trescothick

Champions in 2005, and among the favourites to collect Twenty20 Cup honours in 2008, Somerset were left struggling after three defeats in their opening three games. But then they started to redress the balance. A fine 79 from Peter Trego helped the West Country men to a 15-run win over Glamorgan; Alfonso Thomas's 4 for 27 played a major part in their 10-run win over Worcestershire – they were back in with a sniff of reaching the quarter-finals. Marcus Trescothick shone in the Taunton sun – following a washout against Gloucestershire – hammering a 57-ball 107 in a 67-run win over Worcestershire. The consequences of a four-wicket reverse against Warwickshire at Edgbaston were far from terminal, but then the rain fell. Somerset's last two group matches were washouts and they finished one point behind Glamorgan – who went on to secure a quarter-final berth. Somerset will be keen to get off to a flying start in 2009; they failed to do so in the last Twenty20 Cup campaign, and it cost them.

Batting: Leading Averages in 2008 (qualification: 100 runs)

Player	M	I	NO	R	HS	Ave	SR	50	100
ME Trescothick	8	8	0	306	107	38.25	165.40	1	1
PD Trego	8	8	0	225	79	28.12	122.28	1	0
JL Langer	8	8	0	205	62	25.62	138.51	1	0
C Kieswetter	8	8	1	165	42	23.57	152.77	0	0
ID Blackwell	7	7	0	102	43	14.57	115.90	0	0

Bowling: Leading Economy Rates in 2008 (qualification: 4 wickets)

Player	M	I	O	M	R	W	BBI	Ave	Econ	4w	5w
AC Thomas	8	7	26.2	0	170	11	4/27	15.45	6.45	1	0
AV Suppiah	6	5	14.0	0	110	4	3/36	27.50	7.85	0	0
CM Willoughby	5	5	17.0	0	136	4	2/28	34.00	8.00	0	0
ID Blackwell	7	7	21.5	0	183	4	2/34	45.75	8.38	0	0
ML Turner	8	8	26.0	0	231	9	2/22	25.66	8.88	0	0

Surrey Brown Caps (South Division)
Coach: Alan Butcher
Ground: The Oval, Kennington, London (capacity: 23,500)
T20 Cup 2008 performance: Group stages (P10, W2, L8)
T20 Cup best: Champions (2003)
Star Performer in 2008: Abdul Razzaq

Champions in 2003, runners-up to Leicestershire a year later, and quarter-finalists in both 2005 and 2006; it came as a major surprise when Surrey failed to progress beyond the group stages of the 2007 Twenty20 Cup. Disappointingly, they failed to do much better in 2008. Not one of their batsmen passed the 200-run mark – the benchmark for a steady campaign with the bat; of the bowlers, only veteran Pakistan all-rounder Abdul Razzaq managed to claim more than 10 wickets (he finished with a creditable 15) – it was hardly a recipe for a successful season. Surrey managed just two wins in the 2008 Twenty20 Cup – against Sussex and, surprisingly, against competition runners-up Kent (a game in which Abdul Razzaq took a match-winning 4 for 17) – and finished rooted to the bottom of the South Division table with a dismal four points. It was a season to forget and things can only get better for the South London county in 2009.

Batting: Leading Averages in 2008 (qualification: 100 runs)

Player	M	I	NO	R	HS	Ave	SR	50	100
Abdul Razzaq	9	9	1	185	65	23.12	139.09	0	1
AD Brown	9	9	0	192	51	21.33	147.69	0	1
U Afzaal	10	10	1	187	38	20.77	104.46	0	0
SA Newman	10	10	0	188	52	18.80	133.25	0	1
MR Ramprakash	10	10	0	186	60	18.60	110.05	0	1
JN Batty	8	8	1	122	42*	17.42	110.90	0	0

Bowling: Leading Economy Rates in 2008 (qualification: 4 wickets)

Player	M	I	O	M	R	W	BBI	Ave	Econ	4w	5w
MNW Spriegel	9	9	27.0	0	192	6	2/16	32.00	7.11	0	0
Abdul Razzaq	9	9	32.0	0	232	15	4/17	15.46	7.25	1	0
Saqlain Mushtaq	2	2	8.0	0	64	6	3/24	10.66	8.00	0	0
CP Schofield	6	6	20.0	0	167	7	2/29	23.85	8.35	0	0
JW Dernbach	8	8	27.3	0	244	7	3/32	34.85	8.87	0	0

Somerset – Warwickshire

Sussex Sharks (South Division)
Coach: Mark Robinson
Ground: County Ground, Hove (capacity: 4,000)
T20 Cup 2008 performance: Group stages (P10, W2, L8)
T20 Cup best: Quarter-finals (2007)
Star Performer in 2008: Murray Goodwin

Sussex were looking to the 2008 Twenty20 Cup as an opportunity to build on a 2007 campaign that had seen them produce their best performance in the competition to date – they made it to the last eight of the tournament for the first time. As it was, they lost their first six games and were already out of contention before the competition had really begun. Chris Liddle's 4 for 15 triggered a first win of the season, a comprehensive nine-wicket win over Hampshire; and Murray Goodwin (79) guided them to a six-wicket win over Surrey. But that was Sussex's final taste of victory: three defeats in their final three group games left them above Surrey at the bottom of the South Division table on run-rate. Consistent contenders in recent years in the County Championship, Sussex will be keen to address their dismal record in 20-over cricket. Their squad possesses more than enough talent to do so.

Batting: Leading Averages in 2008 (qualification: 100 runs)

Player	M	I	NO	R	HS	Ave	SR	50	100
MW Goodwin	10	10	2	345	79*	43.12	126.37	0	3
CJ Adams	8	8	2	142	57	23.66	114.51	0	1
DR Smith	10	9	1	185	72*	23.12	155.46	0	1
MH Yardy	10	9	3	129	43	21.50	114.15	0	0
MJ Prior	10	9	0	155	56	17.22	129.16	0	1
CD Nash	8	8	0	101	52	12.62	98.05	0	1

Bowling: Leading Economy Rates in 2008 (qualification: 4 wickets)

Player	M	I	O	M	R	W	BBI	Ave	Econ	4w	5w
RSC Martin-Jenkins	8	8	30.0	1	199	4	1/17	49.75	6.63	0	0
MH Yardy	10	10	38.0	1	273	10	3/24	27.30	7.18	0	0
DR Smith	10	10	35.0	0	297	12	3/14	24.75	8.48	0	0
RJ Hamilton-Brown	10	6	14.0	0	119	4	2/17	29.75	8.50	0	0
CJ Liddle	5	5	19.2	1	165	10	4/15	16.50	8.53	2	0
RJ Kirtley	9	9	29.0	0	305	5	2/16	61.00	10.51	0	0

Warwickshire Bears (Mid/Wales/West Division)
Coach: Ashley Giles
Ground: Edgbaston, Birmingham (capacity: 21,000)
T20 Cup 2008 performance: Quarter-finals (P14, W4, L10, D0)
T20 Cup best: Runners-up (2003)
Star Performer in 2008: Ian Salisbury

Runners-up in 2003 and quarter-finalists in three of the last four seasons, Warwickshire were justifiably high on most people's list of potential Twenty20 Cup winners before the 2008 campaign got underway. And they more than lived up to their promise in the group stages: a tie and a no-result in their first two fixtures were followed by six straight victories. There were standout performances throughout the squad: 19-year-old Chris Woakes took 4 for 21 as they brushed aside Somerset; Jonathan Trott hit an unbeaten 61 in a seven-wicket win over Worcestershire; Ian Salisbury rolled back the years with a match-winning 3 for 18 in the reverse fixture against Worcestershire. With a place in the quarter-finals all but assured, a no-result and a 13-run defeat to Northamptonshire in their final two group games mattered little. But as has been the case in recent years, the quarter-finals proved a step too far: Warwickshire lost to defending champions Kent by 42 runs. It was a disappointing end to what had been a promising campaign.

Batting: Leading Averages in 2008 (qualification: 100 runs)

Player	M	I	NO	R	HS	Ave	SR	50	100
IJL Trott	11	10	3	268	61*	38.28	100.00	0	2
JO Troughton	11	10	1	254	57	28.22	118.69	0	1
T Frost	10	8	1	183	53	26.14	108.92	0	1
NM Carter	11	10	0	208	52	20.80	151.82	0	1

Bowling: Leading Economy Rates in 2008 (qualification: 4 wickets)

Player	M	I	O	M	R	W	BBI	Ave	Econ	4w	5w
AG Botha	11	10	31.0	0	163	14	3/15	11.64	5.25	0	0
IDK Salisbury	10	9	32.0	0	175	15	3/14	11.66	5.46	0	0
CS Martin	11	10	36.0	1	226	9	3/33	25.11	6.27	0	0
NM Carter	11	10	32.2	0	235	8	2/14	29.37	7.26	0	0
TD Groenewald	11	9	25.0	1	218	10	3/40	21.80	8.72	0	0
CR Woakes	11	10	28.2	1	267	7	4/21	38.14	9.42	1	0

The Counties

Worcestershire Royals (Mid/Wales/West Division)
Coach: Steve Rhodes
Ground: New Road, Worcester (capacity: 4,500)
T20 Cup 2008 performance: Group stages (P10, W3, L6, NR1)
T20 Cup best: Quarter-finals (2004, 2007)
Star Performer in 2008: Graeme Hick

Two quarter-final appearances apart, the Twenty20 Cup has not been the happiest of hunting grounds for the New Road men, and although they lifted the National League 40-over title in 2007, they failed to carry any momentum gained into the 20-over game and endured a miserable campaign. They got off to a flying start, as veteran Graeme Hick slammed a 58-ball unbeaten 88 to help his side to a crunching nine-wicket win over neighbours Gloucestershire but, sadly, six matches would pass before Worcestershire could taste success again. Despite two consolation victories in their last three games – over Northamptonshire and again over Gloucestershire – they finished second to bottom in the table. Hick apart – he scored 272 runs, including three half-centuries, in what turned out to be his final Twenty20 campaign – Worcestershire's batsmen failed to fire; as did the bowlers – no side in the Mid/Wales/West group conceded more runs (1,428). It's difficult to see how they will be able to reverse their fortunes in 2009.

Batting: Leading Averages in 2008 (qualification: 100 runs)

Player	M	I	NO	R	HS	Ave	SR	50	100
GA Hick	9	9	1	272	88*	34.00	132.03	0	3
SC Moore	9	8	0	215	51	26.87	147.26	0	1
BF Smith	9	8	1	161	46	23.00	105.22	0	0
VS Solanki	9	9	0	175	51	19.44	109.37	0	2
Kabir Ali	8	7	1	109	28	18.16	129.76	0	0

Bowling: Leading Economy Rates in 2008 (qualification: 4 wickets)

Player	M	I	O	M	R	W	BBI	Ave	Econ	4w	5w
GJ Batty	6	6	22.0	0	143	5	1/11	28.60	6.50	0	0
DKH Mitchell	9	9	30.5	0	205	12	4/11	17.08	6.64	1	0
Kabir Ali	8	8	31.0	1	238	13	4/44	18.30	7.67	1	0
GM Andrew	9	9	30.0	0	252	8	2/20	31.50	8.40	0	0
CD Whelan	6	5	17.0	0	165	7	2/24	23.57	9.70	0	0

Yorkshire Phoenix (North Division)
Coach: Martyn Moxon
Ground: Headingley, Leeds (capacity: 17,000)
T20 Cup 2008 performance: Group stages (P10, W5, L3, T1, NR1)
T20 Cup best: Quarter-finals (2006, 2007)
Star Performer in 2008: Anthony McGrath

Yorkshire started their 2008 Twenty20 Cup campaign off the back of two successive quarter-final appearances, but got off to the worst possible start, losing to Derbyshire and Nottinghamshire in their opening two games. But then came the fightback. A 42-ball 72 from Anthony McGrath helped them to an 11-run win in the reverse fixture against Derbyshire; half-centuries from McGrath and Jacques Rudolph eased them to a six-wicket victory over Leicestershire; and back-to-back victories over arch-rivals Lancashire, coupled with a tie against Durham and a final group game win over Nottinghamshire, seemed to confirm their place in the last eight for the third consecutive year. But then came news that they had fielded an ineligible player against Notts, and they were thrown out of the tournament – moments before their quarter-final match against Durham was due to start. A clumsy administrative error had brought a promising campaign to a premature end. The club will be keen to make amends in 2009.

Batting: Leading Averages in 2008 (qualification: 100 runs)

Player	M	I	NO	R	HS	Ave	SR	50	100
A McGrath	9	9	2	392	72*	56.00	132.43	0	5
JA Rudolph	9	8	1	191	56	27.28	129.05	0	1
GL Brophy	9	9	1	177	57*	22.12	113.46	0	1
AW Gale	9	9	2	106	45	15.14	86.17	0	0
MP Vaughan	7	7	0	104	34	14.85	138.66	0	0

Bowling: Leading Economy Rates in 2008 (qualification: 4 wickets)

Player	M	I	O	M	R	W	BBI	Ave	Econ	4w	5w
RM Pyrah	9	9	30.0	0	209	14	4/20	14.92	6.96	1	0
D Gough	9	9	34.0	0	242	8	2/28	30.25	7.11	0	0
TT Bresnan	9	9	34.0	0	244	8	2/12	30.50	7.17	0	0
AU Rashid	8	7	21.0	0	162	7	4/24	23.14	7.71	1	0
MJ Hoggard	9	9	32.0	1	251	6	2/22	41.83	7.84	0	0

Worcestershire – Yorkshire

Fond farewell: Twenty-five years after his debut, first-class cricket's most prolific run-maker, the Worcestershire Royals' former England batsman Graeme Hick retired at the end of the 2008 season.

Indian Premier League 2009

After all the razzmatazz, hype and media attention of the inaugural season, it seems hard to imagine that the second edition of the Indian Premier League could be as big as the first. But this time round, every side knows its weaknesses: squads will have been strengthened; fans will have developed a closer bond with the franchise of their choice; expectations will be higher. Can Shane Warne's Rajasthan hang on to their crown? Can Bangalore and the Deccan Chargers put their poor 2008 campaigns behind them? What about big-spending Mumbai and Chennai? Will Punjab be the surprise package once again? And will Delhi and Kolkata collect the crown they so covet? Rest assured: the answers are sure to be revealed in spectacular fashion.

Images of 2008:
Main: **Hot property:** MS Dhoni was auctioned for US$1.5million and Chennai Super Kings got good value for their money.
Above: **Moment of Triumph:** Jubilant captain Shane Warne (left) and Sohail Tanvir of Rajasthan Royals raise their bats in celebration after completing the run which signalled their last-ball victory over Chennai Super Kings in the 2008 IPL final.

The Teams

Bangalore Royal Challengers
Owner: Vijay Mallya
Franchise fee: US$111.6 million
Coach: Venkatesh Prasad
Ground: M. Chinnaswamy Stadium, Bangalore
IPL 2008 performance: 7th (P14, W4, L10, D0)
Most expensive player: Rahul Dravid (US$1.035 million)
Star performer in 2008: Mark Boucher

Bangalore's problems in 2008 started the moment their icon player and captain Rahul Dravid decided to base his squad selection on a player's Test credentials rather than on his prowess in the one-day arena. In came Jacques Kallis, Anil Kumble and Mark Boucher and such was the fallout that the franchise's owner, Vijay Mallya, stepped into the mix in the second round of bidding and snapped up Twenty20 specialists such as Misbah-ul-Haq. It was too little too late. Of the big-name players, only Boucher could hold his head up high. Dravid struggled with the bat; Kumble with the ball; and Kallis with both. Bangalore won a paltry four games – with two of those victories coming in the last two games. They struggled for runs – only Kolkata scored fewer – and had no bowling attack, bar the odd standout performance from Dale Steyn, to speak of. Expect big changes to the playing staff if Bangalore are to challenge for honours in 2009.

Activity at Auction
Rahul Dravid (Ind): US$1,035,000; Jacques Kallis (SA): US$900,000; Anil Kumble (Ind): US$500,000; Cameron White (Aus): US$500,000; Zaheer Khan (Ind): US$450,000; Mark Boucher (SA): US$450,000; Dale Steyn (SA): US$325,000; Shivnarine Chanderpaul (WI): US$200,000; Wasim Jaffer (Pak): US$150,000; Misbah-ul-Haq (Pak): US$125,000; Ross Taylor (NZ): US$100,000

Batting: Leading Averages in 2008 (qualification: 100 runs)

Player	M	I	NO	R	HS	Ave	SR	50	100
LRPL Taylor	4	4	0	149	53	37.25	183.95	1	0
MV Boucher	10	10	3	225	50*	32.14	127.11	1	0
R Dravid	14	14	1	371	75*	28.53	124.49	2	0
W Jaffer	6	6	0	115	50	19.16	110.57	1	0
JH Kallis	11	11	0	199	54	18.09	108.74	1	0
Misbah-ul-Haq	8	8	1	117	47*	16.71	144.44	0	0
CL White	8	8	1	114	31*	16.28	111.76	0	0
V Kohli	13	12	1	165	38	15.00	105.09	0	0
P Kumar	13	12	2	112	34	11.20	114.28	0	0

Bowling: Leading Economy Rates in 2008 (qualification: 4 wickets)

Player	M	I	O	M	R	W	BBI	Ave	Econ	4w	5w
DW Steyn	10	10	38.0	0	252	10	3/27	25.20	6.63	0	0
R Vinay Kumar	8	8	23.0	0	182	5	3/27	36.40	7.91	0	0
A Kumble	10	10	38.2	0	304	7	3/14	43.42	7.93	0	0
P Kumar	13	13	44.4	1	366	11	3/23	33.27	8.19	0	0
Z Khan	11	11	42.0	0	357	13	3/38	27.46	8.50	0	0
JH Kallis	11	11	34.2	0	311	4	2/39	77.75	9.05	0	0

Chennai Super Kings
Owner: India Cements
Franchise fee: US$91 million
Coach: Kepler Wessels
Ground: MA Chidambaram Stadium, Chennai
IPL 2008 performance: Runners-up (P14, W10, L4, D0)
Most expensive player: Mahendra Singh Dhoni (US$1.5 million)
Star performer in 2008: Mahendra Singh Dhoni

The Super Kings were the pre-competition favourites for the inaugural IPL season in 2008. They had the best-balanced team, with an array of international stars – Muttiah Muralitharan, Matthew Hayden, Michael Hussey, Stephen Fleming and Albie Morkel – some reliable domestic players and, in Mahendra Singh Dhoni, the golden boy of Indian cricket, an astute captain and one of the most exciting power-hitters in the game. And, for the first four games, at least, they more than lived up to the hype. But when Hayden and Hussey returned to Australia, the team lost three games on the bounce. They may have rallied well, losing just once more en route to the final, only to be edged out by Rajasthan, but they looked less formidable without their impressive Aussie duo. If Chennai are hoping to go one step further in 2009, keeping hold of their best players for the duration of the tournament should be their No.1 priority.

Activity at Auction
Mahendra Singh Dhoni (Ind): US$1,500,000; Jacob Oram (NZ): US$675,000; Albie Morkel (SA): US$650,000; Suresh Raina (Ind): US$650,000; Muttiah Muralitharan (SL): US$600,000; Matthew Hayden (Aus): US$375,000; Mike Hussey (Aus): US$350,000; Stephen Fleming (NZ): US$325,000; Makhaya Ntini (SA): US$200,000

Batting: Leading Averages in 2008 (qualification: 100 runs)

Player	M	I	NO	R	HS	Ave	SR	50	100
MEK Hussey	4	3	1	168	116*	84.00	168.00	0	1
ML Hayden	4	4	1	189	81	63.00	144.27	2	0
MS Dhoni	16	14	4	414	65	41.40	133.54	2	0
SK Raina	16	14	3	421	55*	38.27	142.71	3	0
JA Morkel	13	10	3	241	71	34.42	147.85	1	0
S Badrinath	16	11	5	192	64	32.00	147.69	2	0
PA Patel	13	13	2	302	54	27.45	101.68	2	0
SP Fleming	10	10	1	196	45	21.77	118.78	0	0
S Vidyut	9	8	0	145	54	18.12	133.02	1	0

Bowling: Leading Economy Rates in 2008 (qualification: 4 wickets)

Player	M	I	O	M	R	W	BBI	Ave	Econ	4w	5w
M Ntini	9	9	35.0	2	242	7	4/21	34.57	6.91	1	0
M Muralitharan	15	15	58.0	0	404	11	2/39	36.72	6.96	0	0
MS Gony	16	16	60.0	3	443	17	3/34	26.05	7.38	0	0
JA Morkel	13	13	48.0	0	399	17	4/32	23.47	8.31	1	0
Joginder Sharma	8	7	24.4	0	239	8	2/27	29.87	9.68	0	0
P Armanath	6	6	22.0	0	236	7	2/29	33.71	10.72	0	0

Bangalore – Deccan

Deccan Chargers

Owner: Deccan Chronicle and Media Group
Franchise fee: US$107 million
Coach: Robin Singh
Ground: Rajiv Gandhi Stadium, Hyderabad
IPL 2008 performance: 8th (P14, W2, L12, D0)
Most expensive player: Andrew Symonds (US$1.35 million)
Star performer in 2008: Adam Gilchrist

The Deccan Chargers lived – and ultimately fell – on the belief that Twenty20 is a batsman's game. The money spent on the likes of Andrew Symonds, Adam Gilchrist, VVS Laxman, Scott Styris and Rohit Sharma, left the Chargers' bowling cupboard alarmingly bare; no side conceded more runs in 2008 (2,307). All too often the Chargers took to the field either chasing a big total or knowing they had little chance of defending one – illustrated against Rajasthan, when Symonds scored a majestic unbeaten 117 in Deccan's mighty total of 214 for 5, only for the Royals to win with one ball to spare. On the two occasions the Chargers did win a match– against Mumbai and Chennai – Adam Gilchrist came to the fore (109 not out and 54). If the Chargers are going to lift themselves off the bottom of the pile in 2009, fresh bowling imports will have to be their top priority.

Activity at Auction

Andrew Symonds (Aus): US$1,350,000; RP Singh (Ind): US$875,000; Rohit Sharma (Ind): US$750,000; Adam Gilchrist (Aus): US$700,000; Shahid Afridi (Pak): US$675,000; Herschelle Gibbs (SA): US$575,000; Chaminda Vaas (SL): US$200,000; Scott Styris (NZ): US$175,000; Nuwan Zoysa (SL): US$110,000; Chamara Silva (SL): US$100,000

Batting: Leading Averages in 2008 (qualification: 100 runs)

Player	M	I	NO	R	HS	Ave	SR	50	100
A Symonds	4	3	1	161	117*	80.50	153.33	0	1
RG Sharma	13	12	1	404	76*	36.72	147.98	4	0
Y Venugopal Rao	11	10	2	288	71*	36.00	137.14	2	0
AC Gilchrist	14	14	1	436	109*	33.53	137.10	3	1
VVS Laxman	6	6	1	155	52	31.00	117.42	1	0
SB Styris	8	8	2	112	36*	18.66	91.05	0	0
HH Gibbs	9	9	0	167	47	18.55	109.15	0	0
DB Raji Teja	7	6	0	109	40	18.16	132.92	0	0

Bowling: Leading Economy Rates in 2008 (qualification: 4 wickets)

Player	M	I	O	M	R	W	BBI	Ave	Econ	4w	5w
Shahid Afridi	10	10	30.0	0	225	9	3/28	25.00	7.50	0	0
PP Ojha	13	12	37.0	0	284	11	2/18	25.81	7.67	0	0
DP Vijaykumar	9	9	25.2	0	199	4	1/17	49.75	7.85	0	0
WPUJC Vaas	5	5	17.0	0	145	5	2/9	29.00	8.52	0	0
RP Singh	14	14	51.2	1	442	15	3/35	29.46	8.61	0	0
SB Bangar	11	9	25.0	0	219	4	2/34	54.75	8.76	0	0

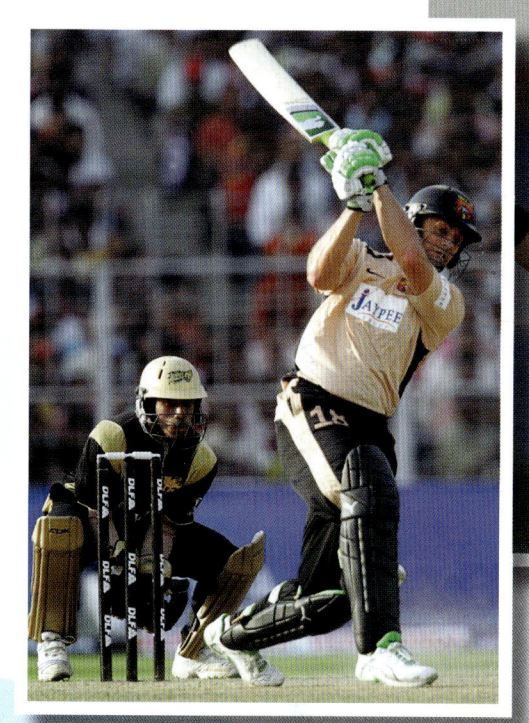

Left and above: **Adam Gilchrist:** The Australian was one of the few bright lights for the Chargers in an otherwise dreadful 2008 season.

The Teams

Delhi Daredevils

Owner: GMR Holdings
Franchise fee: US$84 million
Coach: Greg Shipperd
Ground: Feroz Shah Kotla Stadium, Delhi
IPL 2008 performance: Semi-finals (P14, W7, L6, NR1)
Most expensive player: Virender Sehwag (US$833,750)
Star Performer in 2008: Gautam Gambhir

The Daredevils' blueprint for success in 2008 was to base the side around India's traditional batting strength (in came Virender Sehwag, Gautam Gambhir and Manoj Tiwary) and to use their quota of foreign imports to bolster the bowling attack (with Glenn McGrath, Daniel Vettori, Farveez Maharoof and Mohammad Asif). It was a smart move as it guaranteed the batting line-up would remain undisturbed by international call-ups. The blueprint worked, to a point. Delhi produced a consistent, if not spectacular, campaign. Gambhir (India's best T20 batsman), Sehwag and 22-year-old Shikshar Dhawan shone with the bat and McGrath, a year into retirement, raised a number of eyebrows with his performances with the ball, ably supported by Maharoof. Delhi won seven and lost six of their matches, enough to qualify for the semi-finals, where they came dramatically unstuck against Rajasthan (losing by 105 runs). Consistency is the key for the Daredevils; if they can find it, they will be serious contenders for 2009.

Activity at Auction
Virender Sehwag (Ind): US$833,750; Gautam Gambhir (Ind): US$725,000; Manoj Tiwary (Ind): US$675,000; Mohammad Asif (Pak): US$650,000; Daniel Vettori (NZ): US$625,000; Dinesh Karthik (Ind): US$525,000; Shoaib Malik (Pak): US$500,000; Glenn McGrath (Aus): US$350,000; AB de Villiers (SA): US$300,000; Tillakaratne Dilshan (SL): US$250,000; Farveez Maharoof (SL): US$225,000; Brett Geeves (Aus): US$50,000; Pradeep Sangwan (Ind): US$30,000

Batting: Leading Averages in 2008 (qualification: 100 runs)

Player	M	I	NO	R	HS	Ave	SR	50	100
G Gambhir	14	14	1	534	86	41.07	140.89	5	0
S Dhawan	14	14	5	340	68*	37.77	115.25	4	0
V Sehwag	14	14	2	406	94*	33.83	184.54	3	0
MK Tiwary	9	7	3	104	39	26.00	122.35	0	0
KD Karthik	13	8	2	145	56*	24.16	135.51	1	0
MF Maharoof	10	8	2	125	39	20.83	158.22	0	0
TM Dilshan	7	7	1	104	33	17.33	131.64	0	0

Bowling: Leading Economy Rates in 2008 (qualification: 4 wickets)

Player	M	I	O	M	R	W	BBI	Ave	Econ	4w	5w
GD McGrath	14	14	54.0	2	357	12	4/29	29.75	6.61	1	0
A Mishra	6	6	20.0	0	138	11	5/17	12.54	6.90	0	1
MF Maharoof	10	10	36.0	0	249	15	3/34	16.60	6.91	0	0
R Bhatia	9	9	22.0	0	183	6	2/17	30.50	8.31	0	0
VY Mahesh	11	11	42.1	0	370	16	4/36	23.12	8.77	1	0
P Sangwan	7	7	24.0	0	215	5	2/29	43.00	8.95	0	0
Mohammad Asif	8	8	32.0	0	296	8	2/19	37.00	9.25	0	0

Kings XI Punjab

Owners: Preity Zinta, Ness Wadia, Karan Paul and Mohit Burman
Franchise fee: US$76 million
Coach: Tom Moody
Ground: Punjab Cricket Stadium, Chandigarh
IPL 2008 performance: Semi-finalists (P14, W10, L4, NR0)
Most expensive player: Yuvraj Singh (US$1,063,750)
Star Performer in 2008: Shaun Marsh

Punjab's motto before the start of the tournament was to be "the most successful and entertaining team in the league" and although they may not ultimately have lived up to their own hype, they did show just how far a well-balanced team can go. Under the stewardship of Tom Moody, and captained by Yuvraj Singh, the additions of Kumar Sangakkara, Mahela Jayawardene and Brett Lee were always going to be shrewd ones and the acquisitions of Irfan Pathan, Shanthakumaran Sreesanth and Piyush Chawla were always going to provide consistent performances with the ball. However, it was the form of Shaun Marsh – the son of former Australian opener Geoff – that set tongues wagging. The left-hander's tournament haul of 616 runs (including 115 against Rajasthan) did much to carry Punjab through to the semi-finals, where they ultimately came unstuck against Chennai. However, even though they should retain the services of most of their personnel for 2009, it is hard to see them repeating their 2008 performance.

Activity at Auction
Yuvraj Singh (Ind): US$1,063,750; Irfan Pathan (Ind): US$925,000; Brett Lee (Aus): US$900,000; Kumar Sangakkara (SL): US$700,000; Shanthakumaran Sreesanth (Ind): US$625,000; Mahela Jayawardene: US$475,000; Piyush Chawla (Ind): US$400,000; James Hopes (Aus): US$300,000; Ramnaresh Sarwan (WI): US$225,000; Simon Katich (Aus): US$200,000; Ramesh Powar (Ind): US$170,000; Kyle Mills (NZ): US$150,000; Luke Pomersbach (Aus): US$50,000

Batting: Leading Averages in 2008 (qualification: 100 runs)

Player	M	I	NO	R	HS	Ave	SR	50	100
LA Pomersbach	5	5	4	152	79*	152.00	153.53	1	0
SE Marsh	11	11	2	616	115	68.44	139.68	5	1
KC Sangakkara	10	9	0	320	94	35.55	161.61	4	0
DPMD Jayawardene	13	12	5	179	45*	25.57	136.64	0	0
Yuvraj Singh	15	14	1	299	57	23.00	162.50	1	0
IK Pathan	14	10	4	131	40	21.83	112.93	0	0
JR Hopes	11	11	0	221	71	20.09	149.32	2	0

Bowling: Leading Economy Rates in 2008 (qualification: 4 wickets)

Player	M	I	O	M	R	W	BBI	Ave	Econ	4w	5w
IK Pathan	14	14	53.0	2	350	15	2/18	23.33	6.60	0	0
B Lee	4	4	16.0	0	112	4	1/9	28.00	7.00	0	0
PP Chawla	15	15	46.5	0	389	17	3/25	22.88	8.30	0	0
S Sreesanth	15	15	51.1	0	442	19	3/29	23.26	8.63	0	0
VRV Singh	13	13	48.0	0	420	11	3/29	38.18	8.75	0	0
JR Hopes	11	11	28.0	0	276	7	2/2	39.42	9.85	0	0

Delhi – Kolkata

Kolkata Knight Riders
Owners: Shahrukh Khan, Juhi Chawla, Jai Mehta
Franchise fee: US$75.09 million
Coach: John Buchanan
Ground: Eden Gardens, Kolkata
IPL 2008 performance: 6th (P14, W6, L7, NR1)
Most expensive player: Sourav Ganguly (US$1,092,500)
Star performer in 2008: Brendon McCullum

Kolkata's selections in the first-round auctions were widely lampooned in the media. Unlike Delhi, they decided to base a bowling attack around a core of Indian bowlers (Ishant Sharma, Agit Agarkar, Murali Karthik) and pack the batting with foreign imports (Ricky Ponting, Chris Gayle, Brendon McCullum, David Hussey). The squad contained not a single Indian T20 international. Things got worse. They lost West Indies captain Gayle before a ball had been bowled and, although they got off to a blistering start (led by Brendon McCullum's world-record 158 not out, they hammered the Deccan Chargers in the opening game), the Knight Riders' season did not get going. Icon player and captain Sourav Ganguly struggled; the batsmen failed to fire – no team scored fewer runs (1,845); and the bowlers were left with too few runs to play with. Wins were scarce, Kolkata slumped to sixth in the table, and a change of strategy is needed if they are to reverse their fortunes in 2009.

Activity at Auction
Sourav Ganguly (Ind): US$1,092,500; Ishant Sharma (Ind): US$950,000; Chris Gayle (WI): US$800,000; Brendon McCullum (NZ): US$700,000; David Hussey (Aus): US$675,000; Shoaib Akhtar (Pak): US$425,000; Murali Karthik (Ind): US$425,000; Ricky Ponting (Aus): US$400,000; Agit Agarkar (Ind): US$330,000; Misbah-ul-Haq (Pak): US$180,000; Umar Gul (Pak): US$150,000; Tatenda Taibu (Zim): US$125,000; Mohammad Hafeez (Pak): US$100,000; Salman Butt (Pak): US$100,000

Brendon McCullum: The New Zealand international's star shone all too briefly in 2008, along with those of the rest of his Kolkata Knight Riders' colleagues.

Batting: Leading Averages in 2008 (qualification: 100 runs)

Player	M	I	NO	R	HS	Ave	SR	50	100
BB McCullum	4	4	1	188	158*	62.66	204.34	0	1
WP Saha	12	10	5	159	59*	31.80	133.61	1	0
SC Ganguly	13	13	1	349	91	29.08	113.68	3	0
DJ Hussey	13	13	2	319	71	29.00	123.16	2	0
Salman Butt	7	7	0	193	73	27.57	119.87	1	0
LR Shukla	13	12	4	163	42	20.37	133.60	0	0
DB Das	6	6	0	103	31	17.16	109.57	0	0

Bowling: Leading Economy Rates in 2008 (qualification: 4 wickets)

Player	M	I	O	M	R	W	BBI	Ave	Econ	4w	5w
SC Ganguly	13	7	20.0	0	128	6	2/21	21.33	6.40	0	0
AB Dinda	13	12	39.0	0	260	9	3/33	28.88	6.66	0	0
Shoaib Akhtar	3	3	7.0	0	54	5	4/11	10.80	7.71	1	0
I Sharma	13	13	42.1	1	329	7	1/7	47.00	7.80	0	0
AB Agarkar	9	9	26.0	0	207	8	3/25	25.87	7.96	0	0
Umar Gul	6	6	22.3	1	184	12	4/23	15.33	8.17	1	0
LK Shukla	13	9	12.0	0	124	6	3/6	20.66	10.33	0	0

The Teams

Mumbai Indians

Owner: Mukesh Ambani
Franchise fee: US$111.9 million
Coach: Lachland Rajput
Grounds: Wankhede Stadium, Mumbai; DY Patil Stadium, Mumbai
IPL 2008 performance: 5th (P14, W7, L7, NR0)
Most expensive player: Sachin Tendulkar
Star Performer in 2008: Sanath Jayasuriya

The Mumbai Indians, the IPL's second most expensive franchise, endured a woeful start to their 2008 campaign. Denied the services of icon player and captain Sachin Tendulkar through injury and, following the Sreesanth slapping incident, bereft of the services of Harbhajan Singh after match three for the entire campaign, the Indians lost their first four matches and left themselves with a mountain to climb. Led by veterans Sanath Jayasuriya (514 runs) and Shaun Pollock (economy rate of 6.54 an over), and bolstered by the returning Tendulkar, they rallied well, winning six straight games. But the damage had already been done, and three defeats in the final four matches consigned Mumbai to a frustrating fifth place in the table, one slot short of a semi-final berth. A strong team on paper, and guaranteed the services of Jayasuriya and Pollock for the entire campaign, the Indians could be one of the dark horses of the 2009 season.

Activity at Auction
Sachin Tendulkar (Ind): US$1,121,250; Sanath Jayasuriya (SL): US$975,000; Harbhajan Singh (Ind): US$850,000; Robin Uthappa (Ind): US$800,000; Shaun Pollock (SA): US$550,000; Lasith Malinga (SL): US$350,000; Loots Bosman (SA): US$175,000; Ashwell Prince (SA): US$175,000; Dilhara Fernando (SL): US$150,000

Batting: Leading Averages in 2008 (qualification: 100 runs)

Player	M	I	NO	R	HS	Ave	SR	50	100
ST Jayasuriya	14	14	2	514	114*	42.83	166.34	2	1
RV Uthappa	14	14	5	320	45	35.55	114.69	0	0
SR Tendulkar	7	7	1	188	65	31.33	106.21	1	0
DJ Bravo	9	7	1	178	64*	29.66	132.83	1	0
AM Nayar	14	10	2	206	45*	25.75	149.27	0	0
SM Pollock	13	8	0	147	33	18.37	132.43	0	0

Bowling: Leading Economy Rates in 2008 (qualification: 4 wickets)

Player	M	I	O	M	R	W	BBI	Ave	Econ	4w	5w
SM Pollock	13	13	46.0	1	301	11	3/12	27.36	6.54	0	0
DR Smith	4	4	11.0	0	83	5	3/26	16.60	7.54	0	0
ST Jayasuriya	14	8	21.0	1	159	4	3/14	39.75	7.57	0	0
A Nehra	14	14	44.5	0	348	12	3/13	29.00	7.76	0	0
DS Kulkarni	10	10	29.3	0	236	11	3/33	21.45	8.00	0	0
CRD Fernando	5	5	20.0	0	160	10	4/18	16.00	8.00	1	0
DJ Bravo	9	9	28.2	1	232	11	3/24	21.09	8.18	0	0
Harbhajan Singh	3	3	10.0	0	82	5	3/32	16.40	8.20	0	0
RR Raje	6	6	16.2	0	137	5	2/16	27.40	8.38	0	0

Rajasthan Royals

Owner: Emerging Media Group
Franchise fee: US$67 million
Coach/Captain: Shane Warne (US$450,000)
Ground: Sawai Mansingh Stadium, Jaipur
IPL 2008 performance: Champions (P14, W11, L3)
Most expensive player: Mohammad Kaif (US$675,000)
Star Performer in 2008: Shane Watson

Rajasthan showed that money is not everything in 2008 and made everyone believe that fairy-tales are still possible. Not that you would have known it after their first match, a nine-wicket thumping to Delhi, with a sluggish Shane Warne at the helm. But then the Australian maestro seemed to spring into life, and where Shane dared tread, his Royals team-mates were more than willing to follow. Graeme Smith (441 runs) shone with the bat; Sohail Tanvir (with a competition-leading 22 wickets) and Warne (19 wickets) with the ball; Shane Watson (with 472 runs and 17 wickets) was the player of the season; and the Royals, showing incredible perseverance and a never-say-die attitude, lost only two further games all season and defied the odds to become the Indian Premier League's first champions. The chances are they will not repeat the feat in 2009, but with Warne at the helm, anything is possible.

Activity at Auction
Mohammad Kaif (Ind): US$675,000; Graeme Smith (SA): US$475,000; Yusuf Pathan (Ind): US$475,000; Shane Warne (Aus): US$450,000; Munaf Patel (Ind): US$275,000; Younis Khan (Pak): US$225,000; Justin Langer (Aus): US$200,000; Kamran Akmal (Pak): US$150,000; Shane Watson (Aus): US$125,000; Dimitri Mascarenhas (Eng): US$100,000; Sohail Tanvir (Pak): US$100,000; Morne Morkel (SA): US$60,000

Batting: Leading Averages in 2008 (qualification: 100 runs)

Player	M	I	NO	R	HS	Ave	SR	50	100
GC Smith	11	11	2	441	91	49.00	121.82	3	0
SR Watson	15	15	5	472	76*	47.20	151.76	4	0
SA Asnodkar	9	9	0	311	60	34.55	133.47	2	0
YK Pathan	16	15	1	435	68	31.07	179.01	4	0
Kamran Akmal	6	6	4	128	53*	25.60	164.10	1	0
RA Jadeja	14	9	2	135	36*	19.28	131.06	0	0
M Kaif	16	14	3	176	34*	16.00	102.92	0	0

Bowling: Leading Economy Rates in 2008 (qualification: 4 wickets)

Player	M	I	O	M	R	W	BBI	Ave	Econ	4w	5w
Sohail Tanvir	11	11	41.1	0	266	22	6/14	12.09	6.46	1	1
SR Watson	15	15	54.1	0	383	17	3/10	22.52	7.07	0	0
MM Patel	15	15	55.0	1	420	14	3/17	30.00	7.63	0	0
SK Warne	15	15	52.0	1	404	19	3/19	21.26	7.76	0	0
YK Pathan	16	13	28.1	0	230	8	3/22	28.75	8.16	0	0
SK Trivedi	15	15	48.0	0	399	13	2/25	30.69	8.31	0	0

Mumbai – Rajasthan

Shane Watson: The 2008 Player of the Season used the Indian Premier League to further his claims for a regular slot in the Australian team – and succeeded.

Twenty20 Champions League 2008

The first edition of the Champions League – between the world's best Twenty20 teams – was scheduled to be held in India in December 2008. Then came the terrorist attack on Mumbai and it was postponed. The world's cricket authorities tried to rearrange the tournament for January 2009, but the busy international cricket schedule meant they had settle for October ... with the invitations likely to go to the best teams of 2009.

Television rights for the tournament were eventually sold to ESPN for a staggering US$900 million over a ten-year period. The major beneficiaries of the deal would be the Board of Control for Cricket in India (the BCCI), who would receive 50 per cent of the earnings; the remainder would be split between the two other founding governing bodies – Australia and South Africa. India would play host to the tournament, the winners would receive US$3 million, with each participating side guaranteed a minimum of US$250,000. Either way, we were talking about staggering amounts of money for domestic cricket teams. Just to show that this was very much the BCCI's baby, the argument over player conflicts was resolved in the following way: the two qualifying Indian Premier League sides would have first pick on players.

The 2008 Contenders

Chennai Super Kings (India)
Runners-up in the inaugural Indian Premier League, the star-studded Super Kings, led by Mahendra Singh Dhoni, will be able to call on all of their big guns – Muttiah Muralitharan, Matthew Hayden, Albie Morkel and Stephen Fleming. Having missed out on IPL honours at the final hurdle in 2008, they will be keen to make amends in the Champions League.

Dolphins (South Africa)
They may ultimately have been brushed aside in the final of the Standard Bank Pro 20 series by the Titans, but the Dolphins' reward for reaching their first domestic Twenty20 final is a place in the Champions League. They benefit from not losing any of their players to IPL teams, and in the Amla brothers – Hashim and Ahmed – possess some serious batting talent.

Middlesex (England)
Middlesex claimed their first Twenty20 Cup triumph in impressive fashion in 2008. The most consistent team in the tournament, they have stars in the batting line-up – such as Andrew Strauss – and in Tyron Henderson possess one of the best Twenty20 players in world cricket. The Champions League, however, might just prove a step too far.

Rajasthan Royals (India)
The surprise winners of the inaugural Indian Premier League in 2008, the Rajasthan Royals are a side blessed with quality. Led by the inspirational Shane Warne, and aided by the presence of arguably the world's best Twenty20 player, Shane Watson, they will start the 2008 Champions League as the tournament favourites.

Sialkot Stallions (Pakistan)
Three-time winners of Pakistan's domestic Twenty20 competition, the Sialkot Stallions are the unknown quantity of the first edition of the Champions League. They do, however, possess some quality players, including Pakistan national captain Shoaib Malik and experienced opening bowler Mohammad Asif, who played for the Delhi Daredevils in the 2008 IPL season.

Titans (South Africa)
South Africa's domestic champions may well have to do without the services of both Albie and Morne Morkel (who could be retained by Chennai and Rajasthan respectively), but they still have plenty of talent at their disposal, including Test players AB de Villiers and pace bowler Dale Steyn. They could well be strong contenders for the major prize.

Victoria (Australia)
The kings of Twenty20 cricket in Australia, having won all three editions of the KFC Twenty20 domestic competition, Victoria pose the biggest threat to the IPL teams for Champions League honours. In Brad Hodge and David Hussey, they possess two of the game's leading 20-over exponents, and they also have plenty in reserve in the bowling department.

Western Australia (Australia)
Western Australia made it through to the final of the domestic Twenty20 tournament for the first time in 2007–08, and although they lost out to Victoria, still have a shot at domestic cricket's biggest prize. In Shaun Marsh, a star for Kings XI Punjab in the 2008 IPL, they have the hottest batsman in the 20-over game, but the young opener will have to be at his best if Western Australia are to taste Champions League success.

Man for a crisis: Tyron Henderson was Middlesex's match-winning bowler in the 2008 Twenty20 Cup final.

Glossary

Cricket terminology can be somewhat baffling for those new to the game. Below are some of the terms and phrases you might expect to hear as you watch more and more Twenty20 cricket. Learn them well and, before long, you'll be able to mix it with even the most knowledgeable cricket crowd.

Beamer: a fast, head-high delivery that fails to bounce. An umpire will normally call a no-ball and if a bowler continues to bowl beamers, the umpire will ask the fielding captain to remove him from the bowling attack.

Bouncer: a delivery that is short, fast and which fires up towards the batsman's head. It is a vital part of the fast bowler's armoury, although if the ball bounces too high (i.e. above the batsman's head), then the umpire will call a wide.

Death bowler: a bowler who is an expert at bowling in the last few frenetic overs of an innings.

Doosra: a ball by an off-spin bowler that is delivered out of the back of the hand causing it to turn like a leg break. Meaning "the second one" or "the other one", it was popularized by Pakistan's Saqlain Mushtaq in the 1990s.

Duck: when a batsman is dismissed without having scored a run.

Fine leg: a fielder who fields on the boundary behind square on the leg side of the wicket.

Golden duck: when a batsman is dismissed on his first ball at the wicket without scoring a run.

Googly: a ball delivered out of the back of the hand by a spin bowler (normally a leg-spinner) that turns off the wicket like an off-spinner (i.e. from off stump to leg stump).

Grubber: a delivery by the bowler that simply rolls along the ground after the ball has pitched.

Hat-trick: when a bowler takes three wickets with three successive deliveries.

Hawkeye: the technology used by television companies to track the ball after it has left the bowler's hand; it is particularly useful for determining lbw decisions, and has been adopted by other sports (notably tennis where it is used to verify line calls).

LBW: an umpire will give a batsman out lbw (leg before wicket) if the ball strikes the batsman (usually on the pads) and would go on to hit the stumps. However, a batsman cannot be out if the ball has pitched outside leg stump before hitting him on the pads, or if he has managed to get his pad outside the line of off stump (unless he is deemed not to have attempted to play a shot).

Leg-break: a delivery from a spin bowler that turns from leg stump towards the off stump.

Leg side: the side of the field where the batsman stands when batting; with a right-handed batsman, the leg side will be on the right side of the wicket as you look down at him from the bowler's end.

Maiden: an over in which no runs – except, maybe, byes or leg-byes – are scored.

Off-break: a delivery from a spinner that will turn from the off stump towards leg.

Over the wicket: the bowler delivering the ball with the arm nearer the stumps. For a right-hand bowler, this means he will deliver the ball from the left of the stumps; a left-arm bowler bowling over the wicket will deliver the ball from the right of the stumps.

Popping crease: this runs 4ft in front of and parallel to each wicket. If a batsman does not stand within this area, he could be given out stumped or, if the batsman is completing a run, run out. If any part of his bat or body is on the ground behind the line, he will not be given out.

Reverse sweep: a mirror image of the sweep shot but where the batsman tries to hit the ball through the offside with a horizontal bat.

Round the wicket: the bowler delivering the ball with the arm further away from the stumps. For a right-hand bowler, this means he will deliver the ball from the right of the stumps; a left-arm bowler bowling round the wicket will deliver the ball from the left of the stumps.

Runner: a player who runs between the wickets in the place of an injured batsman. A runner is only allowed if the batsman is injured during the course of a game and with the opposition captain's permission.

Shooter: a delivery – usually by a fast bowler – that stays low after pitching.

Silly mid-off: a fielder who stands very close to the wicket on the off side, slightly forward of square.

Silly mid-on: a fielder who stands very close to the wicket on the leg side, slightly forward of square.

Slog sweep: a more aggressive shot than the sweep. The batsman plants his front foot and swings the bat vigorously to the leg side, usually aiming the ball in front of square leg.

Sticky wicket: a damp surface that leads to the ball bouncing erratically. It is a nightmare scenario for batsmen – who rely on consistent bounce – but a joy for a pace bowler.

Stumped: a stumping occurs when the wicketkeeper breaks the stumps before the batsman is able to ground any part of his body or bat behind the popping crease.

Sweep: a shot played by the batsman in which he helps the ball on its way, rather than fiercely striking it. A right-hand batsman will drop his right leg to drop his body close to the ground and will then swing the bat horizontally to play the ball on the leg side – usually behind square, where the fielding side is only allowed to place two fielders.

Switch hit: when a right-handed batsman switches his stance to that of a left-handed batsman (and vice versa) as the bowler is about to deliver the ball, and proceeds to play a stroke from his new stance.

Wicket-maiden: an over in which neither any runs have been scored by a batsman nor a no-ball or wide delivered by the bowler, but a wicket has been taken.

Yorker: a delivery from the bowler with the aim of hitting the base of the stumps or bouncing inches in front of them. It is a particularly effective delivery against a batsman attempting an attacking stroke.

Twenty20 Rules and Regulations

Number of Overs per Side
One innings per side, limited to 20 overs.

Interval Between Innings
There is an interval of 15 minutes between innings. In the case of a reduced overs match, the interval is cut to 10 minutes.

Time Restrictions
A fielding side has 75 minutes in which to start its 20th over. If a side fails to complete its quota of overs in a given time, the number of overs it receives when batting is reduced by one over for every 3.75 minutes it went over time, except if a side bowls out its opponent in under 20 overs.

Timed Out
An incoming batsman must be ready to take guard at the crease (or be ready so that the batting partner may receive the next ball) 90 seconds after a wicket falls. If not, the incoming batsman will be ruled timed out.

Match Ball
Both sides have to use a white cricket ball.

The Result
Both sides must have faced (or had the opportunity to face) five overs to constitute a match. If a match is weather-affected, the Duckworth-Lewis method is used.

Restrictions on the Placement of Fielders
Fielding restrictions apply for the first six overs of each innings.

Number of Overs per Bowler
A bowler may only bowl a maximum of four overs. In instances where the number of overs in an innings has been reduced, a bowler may bowl no more than one-fifth of the total amount of overs.

Free Hit
If a bowler bowls a front-foot no-ball, the batsman is then entitled to a free hit, whereby he can only be out run out.

Bouncers
Any delivery deemed to have passed above the shoulder height of a batsman will be declared a no-ball.

Over-Rate Penalties
A six-run penalty for each over not bowled in the allotted time will be applied. A bowling side must have started the last of its 20 overs within the 75-minute time frame. Umpires are instructed to apply a strict interpretation of the time-wasting rules with batsmen. If a batsman is deemed to be wasting time, an umpire will dock five runs from a team's score.

Net Run Rate
A team's net run rate is calculated by deducting from the average runs per over scored by that team, the average runs per over scored against that team.

In the event of a team being all out in less than its full quota of overs, the calculation of its net run rate shall be based on the full quota of overs to which it would have been entitled, not the number of overs it faced.

Only those matches where results are achieved will count for the purpose of net run rate calculations. Where a match is abandoned, but a result is achieved under Duckworth-Lewis, for net run rate purposes Team 1 will be accredited with Team 2's Par Score on abandonment off the same number of overs faced by Team 2. Where a match is concluded but with Duckworth-Lewis having been applied at an earlier point in the match, Team 1 will be accredited with 1 run less than the final Target Score for Team 2 off the total number of overs allocated to Team 2 to reach the target.

Statistics: Team and Individual Twenty20 Records

INTERNATIONAL

Highest Total

Total	Team	Overs	RR	Inns	Opposition	Venue	Date
260/6	Sri Lanka	20.0	13.00	1	Kenya	Johannesburg	14/09/2007

Biggest Margin of Victory

By runs

Margin	Winner	Target	Opposition	Venue	Date
172 runs	Sri Lanka	261	Kenya	Johannesburg	14/09/2007

By wickets

Margin	Winner	Balls Rem	Target	Overs	Opposition	Venue	Date
10 wkts	Australia	58	102	10.2	Sri Lanka	Cape Town	20/09/2007

INDIVIDUAL HONOURS

Most Career Runs

Player	M	I	NO	Runs	HS	Ave	BF	SR	100	50
GC Smith (South Africa)	12	12	2	364	89*	36.40	286	127.27	0	3
KP Pietersen (England)	14	14	1	363	79	27.92	244	148.77	0	1
Misbah-ul-Haq (Pakistan)	10	10	5	338	87*	67.60	250	135.20	0	3
A Symonds (Australia)	13	10	4	337	85*	56.16	198	170.20	0	2
PD Collingwood (England)	14	13	0	330	79	25.38	235	140.42	0	2
BB McCullum (New Zealand)	16	16	2	323	45	23.07	269	120.07	0	0
RT Ponting (Australia)	11	10	2	315	98*	39.37	228	138.15	0	2
Shoaib Malik (Pakistan)	12	12	2	313	57	31.30	244	128.27	0	2
ML Hayden (Australia)	9	9	3	308	73*	51.33	214	143.92	0	4
G Gambhir (India)	9	8	0	299	75	37.37	233	128.32	0	4

Highest Score

Player	Runs	Balls	4s	6s	SR	Team	Opposition	Venue	Date
CH Gayle	117	57	7	10	205.26	West Indies	South Africa	Johannesburg	11/09/2007
RT Ponting	98*	55	8	5	178.18	Australia	New Zealand	Auckland	17/02/2005
DR Martyn	96	56	7	5	171.42	Australia	South Africa	Brisbane	09/01/2006
HH Gibbs	90*	55	14	2	163.63	South Africa	West Indies	Johannesburg	11/09/2007
JM Kemp	89*	56	6	6	158.92	South Africa	New Zealand	Durban	19/09/2007
GC Smith	89*	58	11	1	153.44	South Africa	Australia	Johannesburg	24/02/2006
ST Jayasuriya	88	44	11	4	200.00	Sri Lanka	Kenya	Johannesburg	14/09/2007
Misbah-ul-Haq	87*	53	3	5	164.15	Pakistan	Bangladesh	Karachi	20/04/2008
A Symonds	85*	46	7	3	184.78	Australia	New Zealand	Perth	11/12/2007
Nazimuddin	81	50	8	5	162.00	Bangladesh	Pakistan	Nairobi	02/09/2007

Most Career Sixes

Player	Sixes	Innings
Yuvraj Singh (India)	15	6
JPD Oram (New Zealand)	15	8
Misbah-ul-Haq (Pakistan)	15	10
PD Collingwood (England)	15	13
CD McMillan (New Zealand)	14	7
JA Morkel (South Africa)	14	8
ML Hayden (Australia)	13	9
Imran Nazir (Pakistan)	13	9
AC Gilchrist (Australia)	13	13
BB McCullum (New Zealand)	13	16

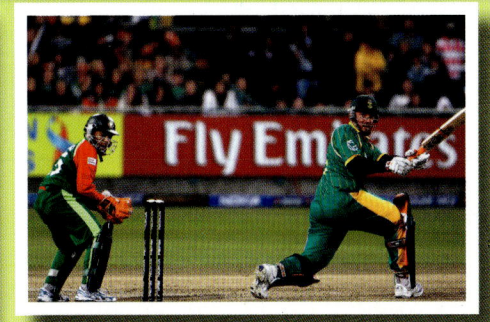

Adding to the total: South Africa's captain Graeme Smith is the leading run-maker in international Twenty20 cricket.

Most Career Wickets

Player	M	O	M	R	W	BBI	Ave	Econ	SR	4w	5w
NW Bracken (Australia)	12	38.5	1	253	15	3/11	16.86	6.51	15.5	0	0
Shahid Afridi (Pakistan)	11	41.3	1	280	15	4/19	18.66	6.74	16.6	1	0
SM Pollock (South Africa)	12	40.3	1	309	15	3/28	20.60	7.62	16.2	0	0
Abdur Razzak (Bangladesh)	9	35.0	1	224	14	3/17	16.00	6.40	15.0	0	0
Umar Gul (Pakistan)	9	33.4	1	181	13	4/25	13.92	5.37	15.5	1	0
RP Singh (India)	8	28.0	0	191	13	4/13	14.69	6.82	12.9	1	0
DL Vettori (New Zealand)	9	36.0	0	203	13	4/20	15.61	5.63	16.6	1	0
SR Clark (Australia)	9	36.0	0	237	13	4/20	18.23	6.58	16.6	1	0
PD Collingwood (England)	14	25.0	0	237	13	4/22	18.23	9.48	11.5	1	0
SCJ Broad (England)	11	42.0	0	355	13	3/37	27.30	8.45	19.3	0	0

Statistics: Team and Individual Twenty20 Records

Best Bowling in an Innings

Player	O	M	R	W	Econ	Team	Opposition	Venue	Date
MR Gillespie	2.5	0	7	4	2.47	New Zealand	Kenya	Durban	12/09/2007
DW Steyn	3.0	0	9	4	3.00	South Africa	West Indies	Port Elizabeth	16/12/2007
RP Singh	4.0	0	13	4	3.25	India	South Africa	Durban	20/09/2007
M Morkel	4.0	0	17	4	4.25	South Africa	New Zealand	Durban	19/09/2007
Mohammad Asif	4.0	0	18	4	4.50	Pakistan	India	Durban	14/09/2007
Shahid Afridi	4.0	0	19	4	4.75	Pakistan	Scotland	Durban	12/09/2007
HS Baidwan	4.0	0	19	4	4.75	Canada	Netherlands	Belfast	02/08/2008
DL Vettori	4.0	0	20	4	5.00	New Zealand	India	Johannesburg	16/09/2007
SR Clark	4.0	0	20	4	5.00	Australia	Sri Lanka	Cape Town	20/09/2007
AR Cusack	4.0	0	21	4	5.25	Ireland	Scotland	Belfast	02/08/2008

Best Career Economy Rate (qualification 10 wickets):

Player	O	M	R	W	BBI	Ave	Econ	4w	5w
JD Nel (Scotland)	19.0	3	85	11	3/10	7.72	4.47	0	0
Umar Gul (Pakistan)	33.4	1	181	13	4/25	13.92	5.37	1	0
DL Vettori (New Zealand)	36.0	0	203	13	4/20	15.61	5.63	1	0
M Morkel (South Africa)	24.0	0	142	10	4/17	14.20	5.91	1	0
Abdur Razzak (Bangladesh)	35.0	1	224	14	3/17	16.00	6.40	0	0
CRD Fernando (Sri Lanka)	28.0	3	181	10	3/19	18.10	6.46	0	0
NW Bracken (Australia)	38.5	1	253	15	3/11	16.86	6.51	0	0
SR Clark (Australia)	36.0	0	237	13	4/20	18.23	6.58	1	0
Shahid Afridi (Pakistan)	41.3	1	280	15	4/19	18.66	6.74	1	0
RP Singh (India)	28.0	0	191	13	4/13	14.69	6.82	1	0

ALL MATCHES

Highest Total

Total	Team	Overs	RR	Inns	Opposition	Venue	Date
260/6	Sri Lanka	20.0	13.00	1	Kenya	Johannesburg	14/09/2007

Biggest Margin of Victory
By runs

Margin	Winner	Target	Opposition	Venue	Date
172 runs	Sri Lanka	261	Kenya	Johannesburg	14/09/2007

By wickets

Margin	Winner	Balls Rem	Target	Overs	Opposition	Venue	Date
10 wkts	Bloomfield	72	86	8.0	Ragama	Colombo	08/10/2005

INDIVIDUAL HONOURS

Most Career Runs

Player	M	I	NO	Runs	HS	Ave	BF	SR	100	50
BJ Hodge	50	47	5	1661	106	39.54	1198	138.64	1	11
HD Ackerman	43	43	6	1463	87	39.54	1209	121.00	1	14
DJ Hussey	59	56	7	1463	86	29.85	1067	137.11	0	9
DL Maddy	48	48	5	1418	111	32.97	1048	135.30	1	11
GC Smith	38	38	5	1265	105	38.33	973	130.01	1	8
M van Jaarsveld	64	59	9	1229	76*	24.58	936	131.30	0	8
GA Hick	37	36	3	1201	116*	36.39	769	156.17	2	10
IJ Harvey	41	40	3	1190	109	32.16	738	161.24	3	4
AD Brown	51	51	1	1170	83	23.40	750	156.00	0	7
MR Ramprakash	44	44	7	1163	85*	31.43	926	125.59	0	8

Highest Score

Player	Runs	Balls	4s	6s	SR	Team	Opposition	Venue	Date
BB McCullum	158*	73	10	13	216.43	Kolkata	Bangalore	Bangalore	18/04/2008
GR Napier	152*	58	10	16	262.06	Essex	Sussex	Chelmsford	24/06/2008
CL White	141*	70	14	6	201.42	Somerset	Worcestershire	Worcester	09/07/2006
A Symonds	117*	53	11	7	220.75	Deccan	Rajasthan	Hyderabad	24/04/2008
CH Gayle	117	57	7	10	205.26	West Indies	South Africa	Johnnesburg	11/09/2007
CL White	116*	53	7	9	218.86	Somerset	Gloucestershire	Taunton	27/06/2006
MEK Hussey	116*	54	8	9	214.81	Chennai	Punjab	Mohali	19/04/2008
IJ Thomas	116*	57	11	7	203.50	Glamorgan	Somerset	Taunton	05/07/2004
GA Hick	116*	65	11	6	178.46	Worcestershire	Northamptonshire	Luton	05/07/2004
Imran Farhat	115	62	13	6	185.48	Lahore Eagles	Tigers	Karachi	01/03/2006
SE Marsh	115	69	11	7	166.66	Punjab	Rajasthan	Mohali	28/05/2008

Statistics: Team and Individual Twenty20 Records

Tough act to follow: Worcestershire will miss Graeme Hick, who retired in 2008.

Most Career Sixes

Player	Sixes	Innings
DJ Hussey	63	56
JA Morkel	55	53
CL White	53	35
T Henderson	53	53
GA Hick	52	36
SB Styris	50	51
LL Bosman	49	30
BB McCullum	48	36
LRPL Taylor	47	24
DJG Sales	47	41

Most Career Wickets

Player	M	O	M	R	W	BBI	Ave	Econ	SR	4w	5w
T Henderson	60	218.2	5	1520	73	4/49	20.82	6.96	17.9	1	0
ND Doshi	44	144.0	0	975	61	4/22	15.98	6.73	14.2	4	0
Yasir Arafat	44	145.1	1	1184	59	4/17	20.06	8.15	14.7	4	0
TJ Murtagh	48	162.1	0	1387	59	6/24	23.50	8.55	16.4	0	1
AJ Hall	40	138.1	3	1086	57	6/21	19.05	7.86	14.5	0	2
CM Willoughby	50	182.5	4	1250	54	4/9	23.14	6.83	20.3	2	0
JA Morkel	64	182.0	1	1389	54	4/30	25.72	7.63	20.2	2	0
J Louw	39	137.4	1	1070	52	4/18	20.57	7.77	15.8	2	0
Azhar Mahmood	48	156.1	1	1169	52	4/20	22.48	7.48	18.0	1	0
SJ Cook	39	139.1	0	1069	50	3/14	21.38	7.68	16.7	0	0

Best Bowling in an Innings

Player	O	M	R	W	Econ	Team	Opposition	Ground	Date
Sohail Tanvir	4.0	0	14	6	3.50	Rajasthan	Chennai	Jaipur	04/05/2008
SR Abeywardene	4.0	0	15	6	3.75	Panadura	Sri Lanka Air SC	Colombo	30/10/2005
AJ Hall	3.4	0	21	6	5.72	Northamptonshire	Worcestershire	Northampton	13/06/2008
TJ Murtagh	4.0	0	24	6	6.00	Middlesex	Surrey	Lord's	23/06/2008
Infanuddin	4.0	0	25	6	6.25	Karachi Dolphins	Sialkot Stallions	Karachi	03/03/2006
MG Dighton	3.0	0	25	6	8.33	Tasmania	Queensland	Toowoomba	01/01/2007
D Mohammed	3.0	0	8	5	2.66	Trinidad & Tobago	St Lucia	Coolidge	02/02/2008
JE Taylor	3.4	0	10	5	2.72	Jamaica	Bermuda	Coolidge	21/07/2006
Iqbal Abdulla	4.0	0	10	5	2.50	Mumbai	Haryana	Ahmedabad	17/04/2007
Mushtaq Ahmed	3.3	1	11	5	3.14	Sussex	Essex	Hove	22/06/2005

Best Career Economy Rate (qualification 10 wickets)

Player	M	O	M	R	W	BBI	Ave	Econ	4w	5w
WA Deacon	28	104.4	3	569	40	4/15	14.22	5.43	1	0
YA Abdullah	17	65.0	0	373	23	3/21	16.21	5.73	0	0
DL Vettori	16	63.0	0	362	21	4/20	17.23	5.74	1	0
HMRKB Herath	16	55.1	1	319	24	3/14	13.29	5.78	0	0
Mushtaq Ahmed	29	98.3	1	580	42	5/11	13.80	5.88	1	1
J Botha	30	105.0	2	621	25	4/19	24.84	5.91	1	0
A Nel	19	70.0	3	418	18	2/13	23.22	5.97	0	0
CK Langeveldt	22	76.0	1	464	32	5/16	14.50	6.10	2	1
D Mongia	32	87.1	1	535	28	3/19	19.10	6.13	0	0
Sohail Ahmed	14	50.4	0	312	25	4/20	12.48	6.15	3	0

Picture Credits

The publishers would like to thank the following sources for their kind permission to reproduce the pictures in this book:

Getty Images: /Doug Benc: 83; /Hamish Blair: 25, 71b, 78, 82, 92; /Duif du Toit/Gallo Images: 26, 87; /Stu Forster: 64, 68-69, 109; /Paul Gilham: 10, 53t; /Laurence Griffiths: 73; /Richard Heathcote: 52; /Julian Herbert: 27, 89; /Sajjad Hussain/AFP: 34; /Alexander Joe/AFP: 71t, 93; /Paul Kane: 90; /Saeed Khan/AFP: 18; /Peter Muhly: 32; /Max Nash/AFP: 48; /Quinn Rooney: 96; /Clive Rose: 119; /Jewel Samad/AFP: 4, 126; /Dibyangshu Sarkar/AFP: 91; /Tom Shaw: 3, 11, 12, 13, 30, 49, 72, 74, 76, 81, 99b, 123; /Sanka Vidanagama/AFP: 84

Global Cricket Ventures: 6-7, 9, 17, 35, 37, 38, 39t, 39b, 41, 43l, 43r, 45, 46, 47, 110-111, 111, 113l, 113r, 115, 117

PA Photos: /Mark Baoveser/AP: 75; /Gavin Barker/Sports Inc: 29, 80; /Jon Buckle/Empics Sport: 55; /Gareth Copley: 51; /Adam Davy/Empics Sport: 62, 86; /Nigel French/Empics Sport: 56; /Themba Hadebe/AP: 15, 21t, 21b, 77, 85, 88; /Daniel Hambury: 54; /Chris Ison: 53b, 63, 98; /Andres Leighton/AP: 50; Tony Marshall/Empics Sport: 99t; /Peter Morrison/AP: 33; /Stephen Pond/Empics Sport: 65, 97, 126; /Aman Sharma/AP: 31; /Neal Simpson/Empics Sport: 70; /Sports Inc: 16, 20, 28, 79; /John Walton/Empics Sport: 58, 61

Every effort has been made to acknowledge correctly and contact the source and/copyright holder of each picture, and Carlton Books Limited apologises for any unintentional errors or omissions, which will be corrected in future editions of this book.